I0820819

Especially for
From
Date

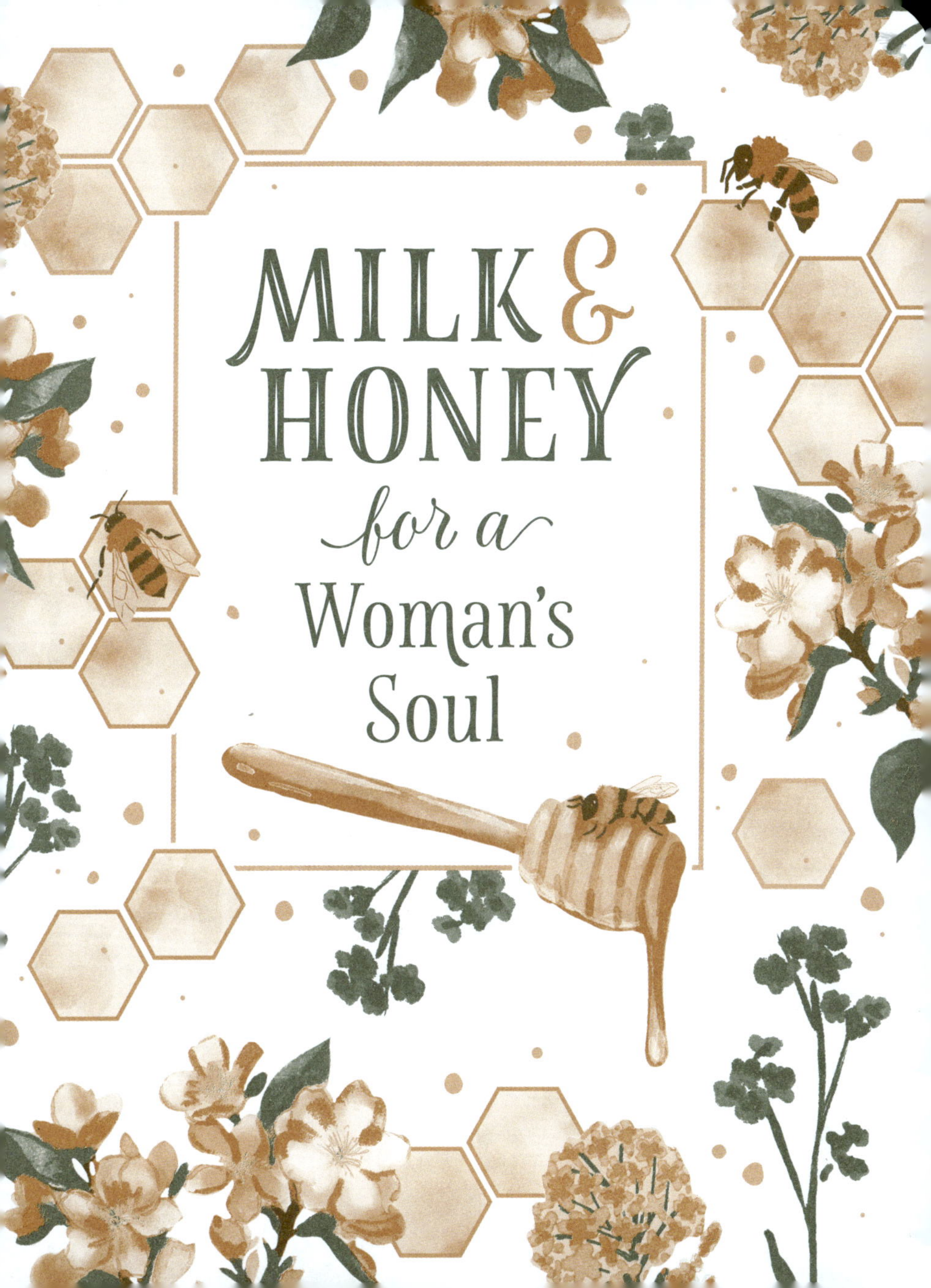
MILK & HONEY
for a
Woman's
Soul

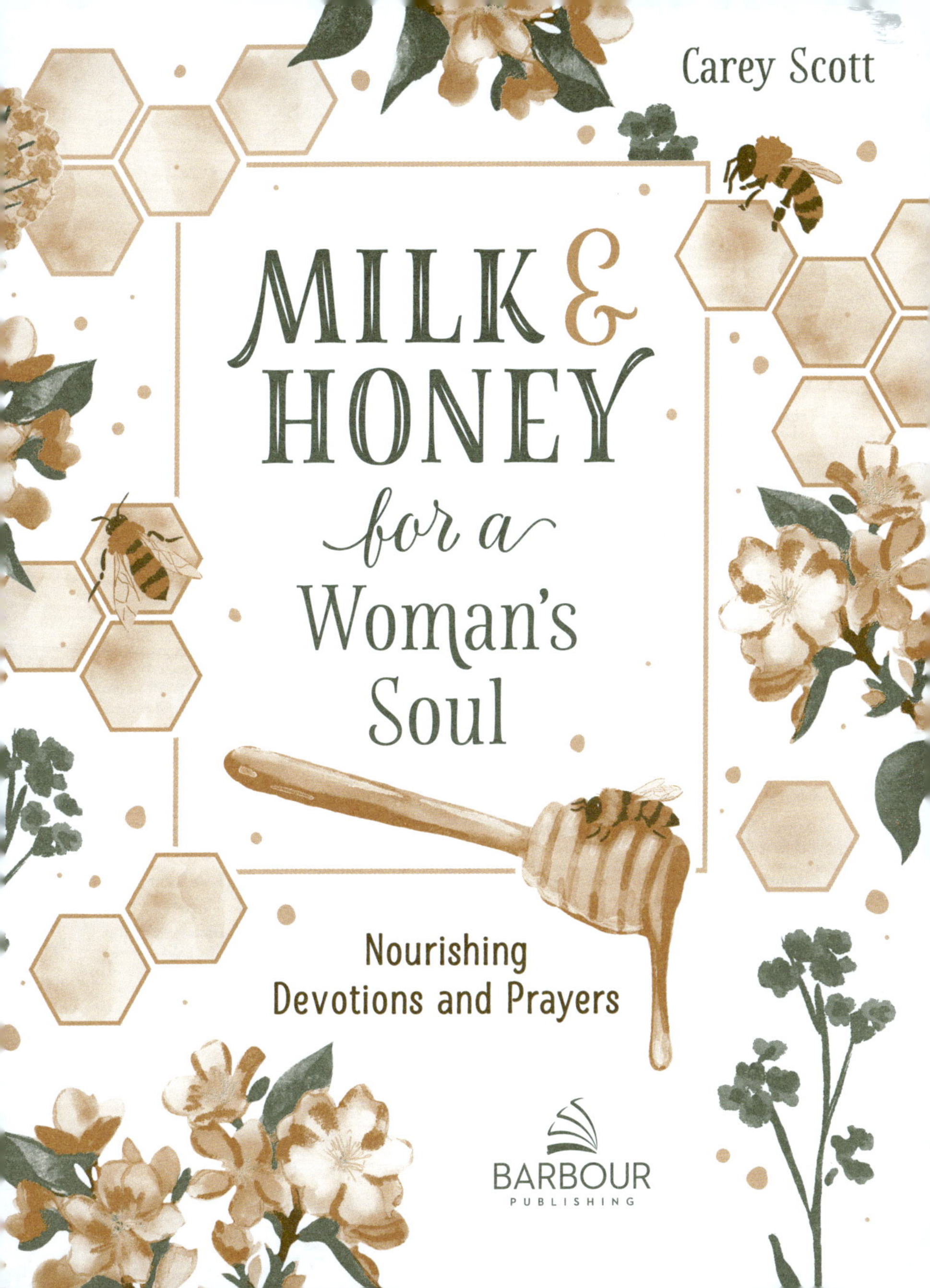
Carey Scott
MILK & HONEY for a Woman's Soul
Nourishing Devotions and Prayers
BARBOUR
PUBLISHING

YOU are the reason we do what we do here at Barbour Publishing. We promise that we will always use our God-given talents to produce content with you in mind—and that we will remain biblically faithful, no matter what.

Thank you for being the heart of our business.

ISBN 979-8-89151-289-4

Cover design: Greg Jackson, Thinkpen Design

Published by Barbour Publishing, Inc., 1810 Barbour Drive, Uhrichsville, Ohio 44683, www.barbourbooks.com

Our mission is to inspire the world with the life-changing message of the Bible.

Printed in China.

INTRODUCTION

Many of us are challenged by trust. We've all experienced moments when someone we relied on didn't keep a promise. We've counted on processes and procedures that fell short. We've placed our hope in institutions, governments, companies, technology, and trendy gadgets that have failed us time and time again—and it's left us bewildered and unsure of whom we can trust.

Knowing that God is a promise keeper in a world full of upsets and letdowns is a game changer! Based on the Bible, we can be confident that He will keep His word and prove His faithfulness. The Lord has kept every pledge He's made and is flawlessly dependable—always has been, always will be. He is trustworthy; you can *always* count on that.

As you spend time with the devotions in this book, your faith will become more anchored in God's promises. Your confidence in His dependability will grow and you'll find comfort in knowing that your trust is safe and secure in the Lord. Your heavenly Father will do what He says He will do.

Go ahead and grab hold of the "milk and honey" promises mentioned in scripture. Let them encourage you as you live out your faith daily.

YOU CAN BE SURE

You can be sure that God will take care of everything you need, his generosity exceeding even yours in the glory that pours from Jesus. Our God and Father abounds in glory that just pours out into eternity. Yes.

PHILIPPIANS 4:19–20 MSG

As believers, we're not left to flounder and navigate life on our own. We don't have to figure everything out for ourselves, work our fingers to the bone, and strive until we're exhausted. Scripture says we can *be sure* that God knows and will meet our needs. While He may not answer in our timing or in the ways we'd hoped, we can trust that our Father's generosity will bless us according to His perfect will.

What needs untangling in your life right now? Where are you falling short? What fears are creeping in and stealing your peace? Keep asking for what you need with an expectant heart. Be confident that you are seen and loved. God will take care of everything you need. Trust His goodness as you wait for divine provision.

Dear Lord, my trust has been broken so many times by people in my life. I confess that I struggle to trust now. Give me the courage to trust You will meet my needs. In Jesus' name, amen.

HE KNOWS IT ALL

The truth is this: You will be in Babylon for seventy years. But then I will come and do for you all the good things I have promised and bring you home again. For I know the plans I have for you, says the Lord. They are plans for good and not for evil, to give you a future and a hope.

JEREMIAH 29:10–11 TLB

Take heart in realizing there's *nothing* God doesn't know. He can't learn anything new. There aren't any circumstances that might catch Him off guard. Nothing can happen behind His back. God is all-knowing, and that is a huge blessing to those who love Him. That wasn't only true in biblical times; it's also true here and now. The Lord has full knowledge and understanding of everything that was, that is, and that is yet to come. We can rest in that beautiful promise.

Your Father was part of every plan He created for you. From your appearance to your gifts to your calling to when you'd come onto the kingdom calendar, God did it all. He gave you a future and a hope, and He is with you every step of the way. Let this comfort you today.

Dear Lord, what a blessing that
You know it all! In Jesus' name, amen.

GOD'S PRESENCE

So don't be afraid. I am here, with you; don't be dismayed, for I am your God. I will strengthen you, help you. I am here with My right hand to make right and to hold you up.

Isaiah 41:10 voice

Anxiety unsettles us when it creeps into our lives. It stirs up our spirits and causes us to worry. We become fearful of the what-ifs. It shuts us down, making us feel overwhelmed and hopeless. As we look down the road, all we see are terrible outcomes and endings. Sound familiar?

What do you do in those moments? Who do you go to for comfort, and what do you reach for to ease your pain and distract yourself? God wants you to know that He promises to be with you in these times. He will strengthen your resolve to weather the storm. The Lord will hold you up so you can hold on to hope. His presence will calm the storm raging inside you.

Go right to God when life gets messy. There's no worldly remedy that's better. A worldly fix may make promises, but it can't deliver. Only He can, and He will.

Dear Lord, You are the solution to my fear and worry. You're the one who can comfort and calm me. Thank You. In Jesus' name, amen.

GOD IS NOT HIDING

"At that time, you will call out for Me, and I will hear. You will pray, and I will listen. You will look for Me intently, and you will find Me. Yes, I will be found by you," says the Eternal, "and I will restore your fortunes and gather you from all the nations where you've been scattered—all the places where I have driven you. I will bring you back to the land that is your rightful home."

JEREMIAH 29:12–14 VOICE

God isn't hiding from you. He's not turning away and ignoring your cries. It may feel like your prayers are falling flat while you're waiting for answers, but God promises that when you pray in earnest, He will listen.

If your marriage is failing or you're tired of being single, call out to the Lord. As you battle to parent a tough teenager or are struggling to get pregnant, bow your head. If your finances are a mess or you receive a scary diagnosis, tell God all about it. When you're overwhelmed by grief or feeling rejected, pray with passion. As you seek Him wholeheartedly, you will be heard and restored.

Dear Lord, help me remember Your promise to hear me and heal me. I will pray and wait with confidence and in expectation. In Jesus' name, amen.

PRECEDENT SET

When the poor and needy seek water and there is none, and their tongues are parched from thirst, then I will answer when they cry to me. I, Israel's God, will never forsake them. I will open up rivers for them on high plateaus! I will give them fountains of water in the valleys! In the deserts will be pools of water, and rivers fed by springs shall flow across the dry, parched ground.

ISAIAH 41:17–18 TLB

Have you ever felt like you were at the end of your rope? All your best efforts to stabilize have failed and you're left feeling defeated. You've tried to figure things out on your own but couldn't. It's in those times, needy and parched, that you cry out to God for help.

There's a precedent set in the Bible. God heard Israel in this condition and answered their prayers. In His great love for them, the Lord provided for their needs with abundance and generosity. If He's done it once, He'll do it again. You can count on it.

As you pray, remind God of instances of His goodness throughout the Bible and ask Him to replicate them in your circumstances.

Dear Lord, I read of Your goodness and am asking You to do it again. In Jesus' name, amen.

GOD'S PROMISES

His divine power has given us everything we need to experience life and to reflect God's true nature through the knowledge of the One who called us by His glory and virtue. Through these things, we have received God's great and valuable promises, so we might escape the corruption of worldly desires and share in the divine nature.

2 PETER 1:3–4 VOICE

God's promises are for those who have a saving faith through Jesus, and He's made them because of His unmatched glory and virtue. They hold great value and worth to believers, reminding us we are free from the lasting effects of this corrupt world. We've been redeemed, and He will transform us through sanctification. Access to God's Word and the work of the Holy Spirit in us give us everything we need to live a righteous life.

What exactly are God's promises? You will find them from Genesis to Revelation as you read the Bible. They include the gift of eternal life (Psalm 23:6), the forgiveness of sins (Acts 10:43), a new heart (Ezekiel 36:26), and rest in your weariness (Matthew 11:28-29). You can trust in every single promise because God is forever faithful. Every divine vow is available to you.

Dear Lord, I know You're trustworthy.
You always do as You say. In Jesus' name, amen.

THE PROMISE OF EVERLASTING LIFE

For God expressed His love for the world in this way: He gave His only Son so that whoever believes in Him will not face everlasting destruction, but will have everlasting life.

JOHN 3:16 VOICE

God loves us so deeply that He couldn't imagine an eternity without His creation. When sin entered the world through the disobedience of Adam and Eve, it brought with it a separation between man and God. His compassion and desire for a restored relationship compelled Jesus, God's one and only Son, to step out of heaven and into the world. His death on the cross paid the price for our sin and forever bridged the gap it caused. It redeemed us. Now, God doesn't see the stains of our transgressions—He only sees the cleansing blood of Jesus that covers us when we ask for forgiveness.

The promise is clear, not only in today's verse but all throughout the Bible. Whoever believes this wonderful truth and accepts this remarkable gift will have everlasting life in heaven. We can be washed clean by Jesus' sacrifice and escape everlasting destruction and eternal separation.

Dear Lord, thank You for making a way and securing my eternal life in heaven. In Jesus' name, amen.

GODLY WISDOM

For in God's deep wisdom, He made it so that the world could not even begin to comprehend Him through its own style of wisdom; in fact, God took immense pleasure in rescuing people of faith through the foolishness of the message we preach.

1 CORINTHIANS 1:21 VOICE

The world is wise in its own eyes. It is quick to offer ideas and solutions that promise short-lived relief. It peddles remedies that look good from a distance but will ultimately disappoint. We know this, yet we still often go to the world first with our problems and put our faith in its pledges.

God offers us His wisdom, and the world can't understand or compete with that. Many of His commands may seem counter-intuitive and even sound silly to earthly ears. Remember that the Lord rescued believers from foolishness by opening our eyes to see His truth. Now we walk by faith and choose to trust that God's way is best. We pray for His direction and guidance. We can capitalize on the promise in James 1:5 that says He will give wisdom to those who ask.

Dear Lord, please share Your wisdom with me today. Help me live with an eternal perspective instead of an earthly one. In Jesus' name, amen.

PROMISED PRAYER ADVOCATE

Meanwhile, the moment we get tired in the waiting, God's Spirit is right alongside helping us along. If we don't know how or what to pray, it doesn't matter. He does our praying in and for us, making prayer out of our wordless sighs, our aching groans. He knows us far better than we know ourselves, knows our pregnant condition, and keeps us present before God. That's why we can be so sure that every detail in our lives of love for God is worked into something good.

ROMANS 8:26–28 MSG

Have you struggled to talk to God, unsure what to ask for? We can't always see the full scope of what we're facing, so we get confused. Our anger or hurt shuts us down. Other times, all we can do is weep in His presence, creating liquid prayers void of words. We're promised an advocate in prayer, especially when we don't know what to pray for or can't find the words.

The Holy Spirit knows exactly what's happening in our lives and hearts. Scripture says He knows us better than we know ourselves. We can trust that when praying doesn't come easy, no matter the reason, the Spirit will speak to God on our behalf.

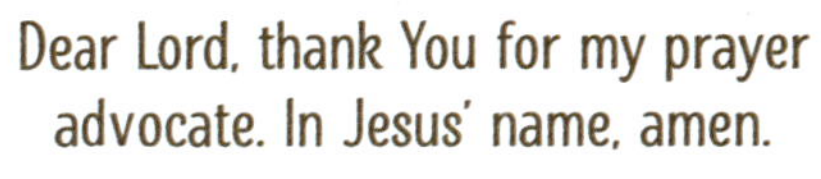
Dear Lord, thank You for my prayer advocate. In Jesus' name, amen.

THE PROMISE TO PURIFY

But if we own up to our sins, God shows that He is faithful and just by forgiving us of our sins and purifying us from the pollution of all the bad things we have done. If we say, "We have not sinned," then we depict God as a liar and show that we have not let His word find its way into our hearts.

1 John 1:9–10 VOICE

Sometimes it's hard to take responsibility for our missteps and wrongdoing. We don't like to focus on our failings and would rather sweep them under the rug. We may disagree when we're called out for mistakes, feeling confident that we are in the right. But we're not perfect, not even close. And while God doesn't expect perfection, He does expect us to own up to our sins.

We are fully forgiven because of Jesus' sacrifice on the cross. His death paid the price for our sins once and for all. But as believers, we still need to confess our sins to God so that nothing stands in the way of our relationship with Him. When we do, God promises to remove the lingering effects of our mistakes, like shame and guilt, and purify us again.

Dear Lord, thank You for the promise of purification from my sins. In Jesus' name, amen.

THE PROMISE OF NO CONDEMNATION

Therefore, now no condemnation awaits those who are living in Jesus the Anointed, the Liberating King, because when you live in the Anointed One, Jesus, a new law takes effect. The law of the Spirit of life breathes into you and liberates you from the law of sin and death.

ROMANS 8:1–2 VOICE

In this letter, Paul tells the Romans about the good news of Jesus and the gift of salvation. He shares God's promise that no condemnation exists for those in Christ Jesus. Living for Christ brings a new way of living that is liberated from sin by the Holy Spirit and leads into righteous living. As believers, this promise is for us too.

Remember that while God doesn't bring condemnation, He does bring conviction through the Spirit. The first leaves you feeling shameful and guilty, while the second prompts you to make changes so your life will align with His will and ways. One leaves you feeling hopeless, while the other fills you with hope for good things to come. Embrace the correction God will bring to those who love Him, trusting that your relationship with Him is forever secure.

Dear Lord, I appreciate how You can correct without leaving me feeling worthless. Thank You for loving me enough to bring holy conviction. In Jesus' name, amen.

WE WILL PREVAIL

When you face stormy seas I will be there with you with endurance and calm; you will not be engulfed in raging rivers. If it seems like you're walking through fire with flames licking at your limbs, keep going; you won't be burned.

ISAIAH 43:2 VOICE

We don't have to navigate the choppy waters of life alone. God promises that when we find ourselves there, He is with us. The Lord will bring calm and strengthen us for that specific storm. While it may seem like we're about to go under, our heads will stay above water when we trust Him. Our situations will be manageable when our anchor is God. The key for believers is to press into Him and persist.

Too often, we allow life to overwhelm us. Instead of standing in faith, we sink in fear and worry. Life is hard, and it only seems to get harder. The world is falling into place for Jesus' return, so we should expect more chaos to ensue. But God promises to be our buoy. With Him, we can endure with hope and expectation.

Dear Lord, it's a relief to know You are always with me and will provide what I need to endure the hard moments. I trust You! In Jesus' name, amen.

A COMPLETE PEACE

A mind focused on the flesh is doomed to death, but a mind focused on the Spirit will find full life and complete peace. You see, a mind focused on the flesh is declaring war against God; it defies the authority of God's law and is incapable of following His path. So it is clear that God takes no pleasure in those who live oriented to the flesh.

Romans 8:6–8 voice

When we train our thoughts on eternal things, we're promised complete peace and a full life. Focusing on God's goodness and the transformative work of the Holy Spirit will calm us. So, when we receive a difficult phone call, discover a betrayal, or our medical tests show something of concern, we need to go right to the Lord. When temptation overwhelms us, we need to open our Bibles and let the scriptures realign us with God's heart. When our minds wander into places they shouldn't, our next step should be prayer. The heavenly Father finds delight in those who keep His commands.

This is called active faith, and the Lord will honor our choice to live righteously. Ask Him for the strength and wisdom to live out this faith so that the promise of peace is realized.

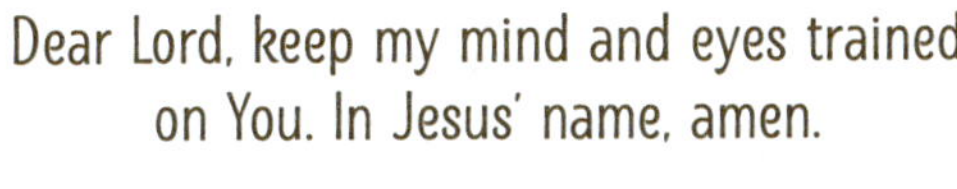

Dear Lord, keep my mind and eyes trained on You. In Jesus' name, amen.

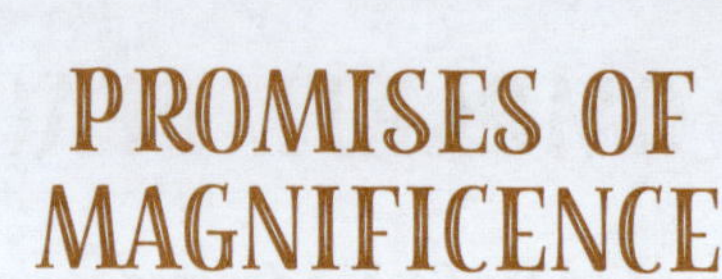

PROMISES OF MAGNIFICENCE

I am the Lord, who opened a way through the waters, making a path right through the sea. I called forth the mighty army of Egypt with all its chariots and horses, to lie beneath the waves, dead, their lives snuffed out like candlewicks. But forget all that—it is nothing compared to what I'm going to do!

Isaiah 43:16–18 TLB

God reminds us of His might and power, and what was accomplished in the wilderness. The Israelites couldn't imagine the miracle of the Red Sea splitting and allowing them to cross through on dry ground. They just saw the sea before them and an enemy behind. But the Lord miraculously made a way, bringing the Israelites to safety and closing the waters on the Egyptians. This is representative of what He can do! We are promised that this magnificent act of God is nothing compared to what's next.

As believers, our takeaway is that we should expect big things. God promises them! There's nothing impossible for Him. So, don't be afraid to ask for something grandiose. Be bold in your requests and pray with expectation.

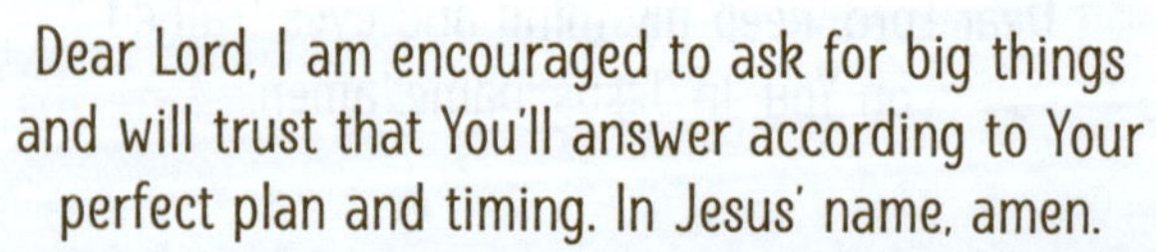

Dear Lord, I am encouraged to ask for big things and will trust that You'll answer according to Your perfect plan and timing. In Jesus' name, amen.

SAY GOODBYE TO THE FLESH

If the Spirit of the One who resurrected Jesus from the dead lives inside of you, then you can be sure that He who raised Him will cast the light of life into your mortal bodies through the life-giving power of the Spirit residing in you. So, my brothers and sisters, you owe the flesh nothing! You do not need to live according to its ways, so abandon its oppressive regime.

ROMANS 8:11–12 VOICE

You owe the flesh nothing! This is a powerful encouragement to be more eternally focused rather than feeding your earthly desires. This is often a difficult choice to make.

It means you forgive instead of holding a grudge, even when you're in the right. You stop engaging with entertainment that pulls you away from God. You don't gossip or boast. When jealousy creeps in, you step away from social media. You exhibit self-control over your tongue when someone makes you mad. And you show love and compassion rather than having a critical spirit.

Now that the Spirit is living in you, God promises He will guide and lead you to live in holy ways that are good for you and will glorify Him. Say goodbye to the oppressive regime of your flesh

Dear Lord, I will choose faith over flesh!
In Jesus' name, amen.

THE PROMISE OF FORGIVENESS

I, yes, I alone am he who blots away your sins for my own sake and will never think of them again. Oh, remind me of this promise of forgiveness, for we must talk about your sins. Plead your case for my forgiving you. From the very first your ancestors sinned against me—all your forebears transgressed my law.

ISAIAH 43:25–27 TLB

When God promises to *blot away your sins* and *never think of them again*, He means it. You are washed clean by the blood of Jesus, and every transgression you have made or will ever commit has been removed from your record. Without the Lord's forgiveness, that record would be miles long—and we, in our own strength, could never overcome it.

Sit with God in gratitude today. Thank Him for making a way through Jesus' work on the cross and for desiring reconciliation with you. Be grateful that once you come into a saving faith and you've been forgiven for all sins, you are always and forever forgiven. Thank God for His unshakable Word and ensuring every promise made is a promise kept.

Dear Lord, You are a good, good Father! My heart is full of thanksgiving as I think of how You've blessed me. Thank You especially for the promise of forgiveness. In Jesus' name, amen.

THE PROMISED INHERITANCE

Through that prayer, God's Spirit confirms in our spirits that we are His children. If we are God's children, that means we are His heirs along with the Anointed, set to inherit everything that is His. If we share His sufferings, we know that we will ultimately share in His glory.

ROMANS 8:16–17 VOICE

In today's verses, Paul sets our expectations as believers. John 1:12 explains that we are God's children; therefore, we will share in Christ's sufferings now and will share in His glory later. We are co-heirs with Jesus, so what belongs to Him will also belong to us. Galatians 4:7 says, "You no longer have to live as a slave because you are a child of God. And since you are His child, God guarantees an inheritance is waiting for you." That is a solid and irrevocable promise.

We were once far away and adrift in our sins, but Jesus changed that. Through His blood shed on the cross, we're secured in His family once and for all. Today, we are blessed to experience God's goodness here on earth, knowing that the promise of an eternal inheritance is to come.

Dear Lord, I'm humbled to be considered a co-heir with Jesus. Thank You for including me in both Your sufferings and glory. In Jesus' name, amen.

OUR HEART'S DESIRE

Be delighted with the Lord. Then he will give you all your heart's desires. Commit everything you do to the Lord. Trust him to help you do it, and he will.

PSALM 37:4–5 TLB

When you choose to savor your relationship with God, dedicate your day to Him, and believe He will empower you step by step, there's a promise attached. Being all in with God allows us to experience blessings in abundance. Scripture clearly says He will give us our heart's desires.

But be careful! This doesn't mean the Lord will automatically supply your earthly cravings, like a new car, a bigger home, extravagant vacations, unlimited funds, or the perfect boyfriend or husband. God is not a genie in a bottle, ready and willing to grant your worldly wishes when you ask. Consider that as you deepen your connection with the Lord, your heart will begin to change. Your desires will change. Your heart will want the things of the Spirit, like wisdom, comfort, strength, compassion, and the ability to forgive. These will become your greatest longings, because your heart will align with God's.

Dear Lord, help me strengthen my faith by trusting You and inviting You into my day. I want for me what You want for me. Sync my heart to Yours. In Jesus' name, amen.

THE PROMISED TIME

Yet what we suffer now is nothing compared to the glory he will give us later. For all creation is waiting patiently and hopefully for that future day when God will resurrect his children. For on that day thorns and thistles, sin, death, and decay—the things that overcame the world against its will at God's command—will all disappear, and the world around us will share in the glorious freedom from sin which God's children enjoy.

ROMANS 8:18–21 TLB

Today's verses share the promise that better days are ahead for the believer. While here, we will suffer heartaches in every area of our lives. We will battle insecurities that threaten to overwhelm us. There will be times of betrayal that we never saw coming. We will have to navigate grief and sadness. We'll have to deal with the sting of rejection and the pain of abandonment. The state of the nation and the world will create fear, and trying to raise godly kids will create worry. The simple truth is that every one of us will suffer. But better days are coming.

All of creation waits with expectation for that promised time when we will be face-to-face with God.

Dear Lord, thank You for the promise of glorious days ahead. In Jesus' name, amen.

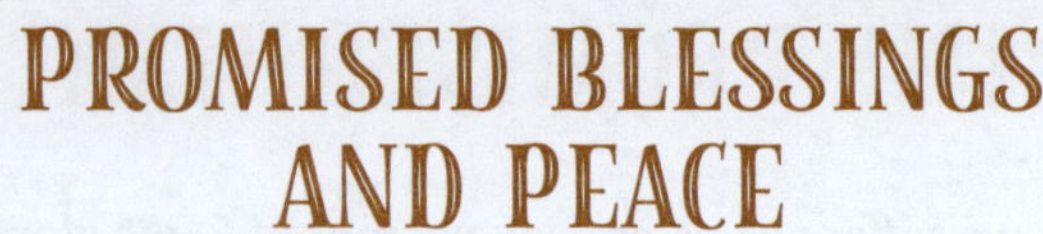

PROMISED BLESSINGS AND PEACE

Stop your anger! Turn off your wrath. Don't fret and worry—it only leads to harm. For the wicked shall be destroyed, but those who trust the Lord shall be given every blessing. Only a little while and the wicked shall disappear. You will look for them in vain. But all who humble themselves before the Lord shall be given every blessing and shall have wonderful peace.

PSALM 37:8–11 TLB

The psalmist reminds us that believers are to trust God and humble themselves in His presence. This may sound simple on paper but living it out each day requires great intentionality. Our default is to trust ourselves first and foremost. We often believe that our education and life experiences make us experts. But nothing earthly is greater than God's divinity.

If we obey, we are promised abundant blessings and supernatural peace. We will reap the rewards for actively sowing into our relationship with the Lord. Every time we choose to trust rather than stress or worry, He will take note. God sees when we choose to surrender our control into His hands. He will give us what's promised.

Dear Lord, help me trust You in my circumstances and be meek in Your presence so I can experience blessings and peace. In Jesus' name, amen.

HE IS COMING BACK

For we know that all creation groans in unison with birthing pains up until now. And there is more; it's not just creation—all of us are groaning together too. Though we have already tasted the firstfruits of the Spirit, we are longing for the total redemption of our bodies that comes when our adoption as children of God is complete.

ROMANS 8:22–23 VOICE

Have you ever been in a tough situation where you threw your hands up and said, "Come, Lord Jesus!"? Or have you heard about the terrible atrocities happening around the globe and longed to be in heaven instead? Maybe after receiving bad news or losing someone dear to you, your tears were liquid prayers pleading for God to rescue you from pain. These are examples of the groans we are experiencing as His creation. We long for our promised eternal life in heaven, without the cares of this world weighing us down.

You can trust that He is coming back! He said He would, and our God will fulfill every vow made to His children. Be hopeful and live with joyful expectancy for the Lord's return.

Dear Lord, knowing You're coming back for me gives me peace and comfort. This life is a breath, and I'll occupy it faithfully until You return. In Jesus' name, amen.

GOD SEES OUR DEEDS

Day by day the Lord observes the good deeds done by godly men, and gives them eternal rewards. He cares for them when times are hard; even in famine, they will have enough.

PSALM 37:18–19 TLB

God is always watching us. He knows our thoughts and what weighs on our hearts. He sees how we treat the people we love as well as complete strangers. He understands our motives and why we react and respond the way we do. The Lord is all knowing, all the time.

When we are compassionate toward others, God logs our actions in the heavens. We collect eternal rewards when we choose to love the unlovable, treating them with care and respect. When we decide to extend grace and forgive the unforgivable, blessings are stored up for us in glory. The Lord promises to care for and provide for believers when we face hard times in our work and personal lives here on earth. Our pursuit of righteous living is richly rewarded by our proud Father, who knows the difficult choices that were made. He promises to bless us for doing good.

Dear Lord, I want to make You proud in the ways I live my life here on earth. Empower me to be a blessing to those around me. In Jesus' name, amen.

INSEPARABLE

But no matter what comes, we will always taste victory through Him who loved us. For I have every confidence that nothing—not death, life, heavenly messengers, dark spirits, the present, the future, spiritual powers, height, depth, nor any created thing—can come between us and the love of God revealed in the Anointed, Jesus our Lord.

ROMANS 8:37–39 VOICE

Today, find comfort in knowing there is nothing—absolutely *nothing*—that can separate you from God's love. This is a bold promise from the one who created you and sees your immeasurable value. His love is unconditional and unshakable. This is refreshing because this world's love is often full of conditions.

No matter how many times you mess up, no matter the seasons of sin that trap you, no matter how often you stumble in your efforts to live well, God's love never changes. It's immovable. Even when He's unhappy about your disobedience or rebellion, none of that affects His care and compassion. The reality is that He cannot love you any more or any less than He does right now. You can always count on His love to be steady and stable.

Dear Lord, it's a blessing and a relief to know Your love for me isn't dependent on anything I do or don't do. In Jesus' name, amen.

BEING RIGHT WITH GOD

If you are right with God, He strengthens you for the journey; the Eternal will be pleased with your life. And even though you trip up, you will not fall on your face because He holds you by the hand.

PSALM 37:23–24 VOICE

God isn't looking for perfection. He doesn't expect us to manage our Christian life flawlessly. But as believers, we're not to live carelessly or be reckless with our choices either. Instead, we are called to seek His help daily. We need it! With worldly forces pushing in and evil all around, we desperately need God to empower us with wisdom, discernment, peace, and strength. We need His hand to guide our next steps. He promises to give us His divinity—we need it to override our humanity. As we follow His commands for righteous living, it will please the Lord.

This life isn't easy. We will fall. We will fail regardless of our best efforts. We will give in to our fleshly desires even when we know better. But we can also repent, take God's extended hand of forgiveness, and try again.

Dear Lord, help me live in ways that are good for me and bring You glory. Strengthen me to live with purpose. In Jesus' name, amen.

WE CAN STAND STRONG

But the Lord will not let these evil men succeed, nor let the godly be condemned when they are brought before the judge. Don't be impatient for the Lord to act! Keep traveling steadily along his pathway and in due season he will honor you with every blessing, and you will see the wicked destroyed.

PSALM 37:33–34 TLB

Be encouraged! This promise is designed to help you stand strong against the enemy—be it the devil's plans or the mean-spiritedness of others. Regardless of what or who, God won't just stand by without a divine response. He's not okay with how you're being treated. Your heavenly Father doesn't appreciate the condemnation that's flooding your heart. So, take a deep breath and trust that He will exact judgment in His timing. Let's not allow ourselves to become impatient as we wait for His intervention. God knows what He's doing. His plans are perfect, and His timing is impeccable.

Until then, we need to continue moving forward and trust that every wrong will be made right. He will take care of us. We can be patient because we know this to be true.

Dear Lord, thank You for being my defender.
Thank You for stepping in when I'm treated poorly.
I love You so much. In Jesus' name, amen.

YOUR PROMISED REFUGE

The Lord saves the godly! He is their salvation and their refuge when trouble comes. Because they trust in him, he helps them and delivers them from the plots of evil men.

PSALM 37:39–40 TLB

As believers, we can have full confidence that God will always be our safe place in troubled times. When your relationship is falling apart and you can't fix it, He is your refuge. When your adult child is making heartbreaking decisions and won't listen to reason, the Lord is your sanctuary. When the medical treatment is failing and you're scared for what's ahead, He's your shelter. When bankruptcy is your only option, He will be your retreat. He promises to save the godly. While it may look different than what we prayed for, the Lord's vow still remains true.

There is no better place to sink your trust than in God. You may be deeply loved by your family, have amazing friends, and be surrounded by a good and godly church family, but they can't deliver you from trouble like He can. Let the Lord be your asylum, just as He promised to be.

Dear Lord, bolster my confidence so I can trust in You alone to be my salvation and safe place. In Jesus' name, amen.

PERFECT TRACK RECORD

The time has come for me to die and return to the earth. But I want to leave you with these thoughts: Think back and you will know without a doubt that not one single good thing that the Eternal One, your God, promised you has been left undone. Not a single one.

JOSHUA 23:14 VOICE

Joshua knew his time was short and wanted to encourage those left behind to be strong in their belief and faith. They were challenged to look back on the promises God had made and the promises He had kept, noting *not even one* was left undone. Imagine how this powerful reminder strengthened their faith as they said goodbye to Joshua.

What do you see when you look back on God's hand in your life? You may be waiting for Him to act in some circumstances, but where have you seen His promises come to pass so far? The Lord has a perfect track record in your life. Every promise made is a promise He has—or will—bring to fruition according to His plan. God is always faithful, and He will continue to be forever.

Dear Lord, Your track record of keeping promises is flawless. I know I can trust You in every way. In Jesus' name, amen.

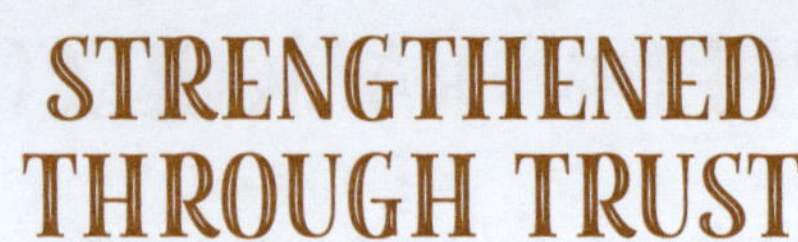

STRENGTHENED THROUGH TRUST

But those who trust in the Eternal One will regain their strength. They will soar on wings as eagles. They will run—never winded, never weary. They will walk—never tired, never faint.

Isaiah 40:31 voice

If you trust in God and press into Him as your source, your strength will be restored. You will have the energy for whatever life brings your way. You may feel overwhelmed, but you won't be overcome. You may feel the weight of your circumstances, but they won't weigh you down. There's a supernatural transaction that takes place. You lay your burdens at His feet, and He strengthens yours to move forward. As a believer, it's a win-win all the way around.

What keeps you from going right to God when times get tough? Why do you work so hard in your own strength, even knowing the extent of your human limitations? Think about it. When have your ways ever bested God's? The reality is that they haven't, and they never will.

If you're serious about your walk with Jesus and want to be empowered to thrive in your divine calling, your only option is daily reliance on the Lord.

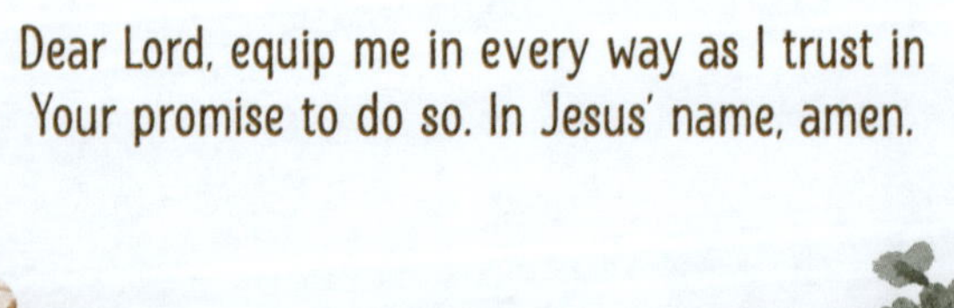

Dear Lord, equip me in every way as I trust in Your promise to do so. In Jesus' name, amen.

GOD'S WORD IS EVERLASTING

The grass withers, the flower fades as the breath of the Eternal One blows away. People are no different from grass. The grass withers, the flower fades; nothing lasts except the word of our God. It will stand forever.

ISAIAH 40:7–8 VOICE

Everything the world produces is temporary. It will eventually spoil, rust, stop working, go out of style, or disintegrate. Even as we may seek the fountain of youth in one way or another, we too will pass away. But God promises that His Word will stand forever.

We see that as we dig through scripture, understanding that who He was back in the day is the same God we worship here and now. He will be the same for future generations as well. He's unchanging, and His love for us stands strong and unmoved. His Word is unaffected by time and space. Wars and weather don't change it. Social trends can't change it. It's everlasting, and that's a promise from God.

Dig into scripture and be confident that what you find is real and true. The written Word is His love letter, revealing Himself to you in meaningful ways. Spend time in it every day and let the Lord encourage you.

Dear Lord, thank You for Your enduring Word! In Jesus' name, amen.

PROMISED PEACE

Don't worry about anything; instead, pray about everything; tell God your needs, and don't forget to thank him for his answers. If you do this, you will experience God's peace, which is far more wonderful than the human mind can understand. His peace will keep your thoughts and your hearts quiet and at rest as you trust in Christ Jesus.

PHILIPPIANS 4:6–7 TLB

Want to experience God's supernatural peace right now? When you choose to pray rather than worry about your circumstances, that's exactly what happens. Talking to God brings calm to the chaos. Losing your job, filing for bankruptcy, receiving a scary diagnosis, filing for divorce, navigating infertility, and discovering betrayal are gut punches that leave us anxious and fearful. Let these messy moments be what drives you to pray.

Only God can quiet your mind and heart so you can find your footing. He is the one who will strengthen you to stand as the storms hit. He will settle your spirit. It's a guaranteed promise from the Lord.

The world cannot bring lasting peace and rest for the weary. It is no replacement for God's everlasting love and promises. When life stirs you up, pray.

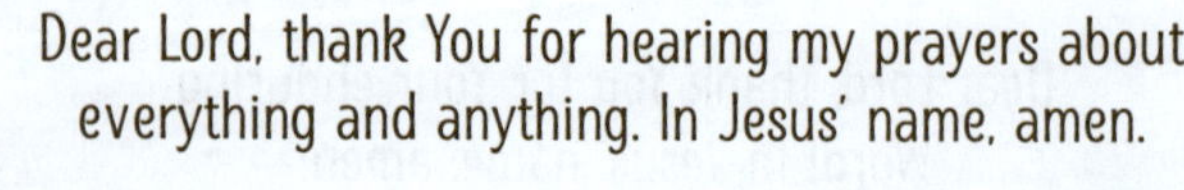
Dear Lord, thank You for hearing my prayers about everything and anything. In Jesus' name, amen.

FIXING YOUR THOUGHTS

And now, brothers, as I close this letter, let me say this one more thing: Fix your thoughts on what is true and good and right. Think about things that are pure and lovely, and dwell on the fine, good things in others. Think about all you can praise God for and be glad about. Keep putting into practice all you learned from me and saw me doing, and the God of peace will be with you.

PHILIPPIANS 4:8–9 TLB

The Bible talks a lot about peace, and God's promises regarding this topic abound. He knows the troubles this life will bring. He's aware of the chaos and confusion we'll experience. The Lord sees the plot twists coming our direction, and He understands how they will unravel us. He knows the heartache headed our way. God recognizes the situations that will shake and break us. That's why we're instructed to keep our minds focused on the right things. Hardships will come, but we can find peace in them.

Grab on to His promise to keep your heart in harmony. Don't sit in those moments and spin out of control. God will help you find stability if you'll put into practice what today's verses prescribe.

Dear Lord, fix my thoughts on what's good and right. In Jesus' name, amen.

A HOLY CONFIDENCE

I know how to live on almost nothing or with everything.
I have learned the secret of contentment in every situation,
whether it be a full stomach or hunger, plenty or want;
for I can do everything God asks me to with the help
of Christ who gives me the strength and power.
PHILIPPIANS 4:12–13 TLB

Paul understood this truth at his core. He knew that walking out God's calling on his life was doable because the Lord would equip Paul for it. That also meant he understood that without God's help, it would be impossible. This apostle had a holy confidence we should pray for today.

As we trust God's promise to be our source, we'll find the strength to do whatever is asked. Whether we share our testimony on a public stage, travel the world as missionaries, lead a Bible study, volunteer, or focus on raising a family of faith, He will enable us. No matter if the task before us is difficult or feels completely in our wheelhouse, God will equip us with the tools we need to obey.

Dear Lord, give me a holy confidence to know that if You call me to something, You will give me the tools to obey. I can do everything You ask with Your help. In Jesus' name, amen.

THE PROMISE OF WISDOM

If you don't have all the wisdom needed for this journey, then all you have to do is ask God for it; and God will grant all that you need. He gives lavishly and never scolds you for asking. The key is that your request be anchored by your single-minded commitment to God. Those who depend only on their own judgment are like those lost on the seas, carried away by any wave or picked up by any wind.

JAMES 1:5–6 VOICE

God's wisdom is a necessary tool for believers to navigate this life. He knows the details of every circumstance and the complexity of every emotion. He gives us the knowledge we need to move forward with purpose. We may be intuitive and have lots of good life experiences to draw from, but nothing can top God's understanding. This is why we must ask for it every day. Leaning on our own understanding is going into a situation partially blind.

Take God up on His promise. He welcomes your requests for wisdom with open arms. Rather than trusting yourself or the advice of those around you, seek His ways through scripture and prayer.

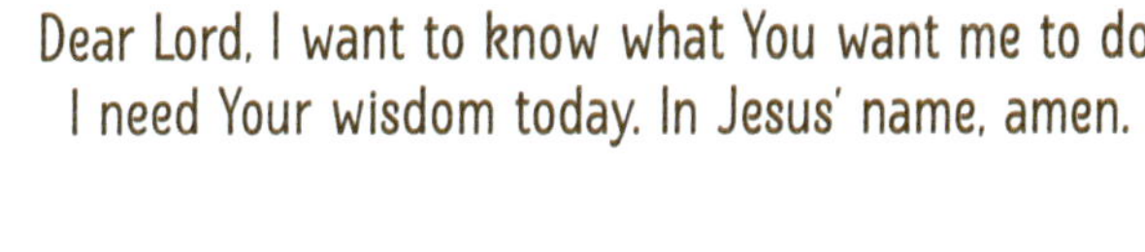

Dear Lord, I want to know what You want me to do.
I need Your wisdom today. In Jesus' name, amen.

AN ETERNAL REWARD

Happy is the person who can hold up under the trials of life. At the right time, he'll know God's sweet approval and will be crowned with life. As God has promised, the crown awaits all who love Him.

JAMES 1:12 VOICE

The heavenly crown is a promise to believers who love God and trust Him, faithfully enduring every earthly test and trial. It's a recognition of spiritual victory. It's given for having the perseverance to stand strong through the storms of life. We can be confident that God has prepared a bouquet of blessings for those of us who have suffered. We can be happy knowing we've demonstrated our love for the Lord through our committed endurance. An eternal reward awaits.

Think of the trials you're currently facing. Maybe you've discovered a betrayal or are working through feelings of rejection. Perhaps your dreams have been dashed. Has someone been careless with your emotions? Has there been a breakdown in your relationship, or do you feel like a failure in your parenting? Are you in the midst of a health crisis? These are the moments we must press into the Lord for hope and help, trusting He will bring us safely through to the other side.

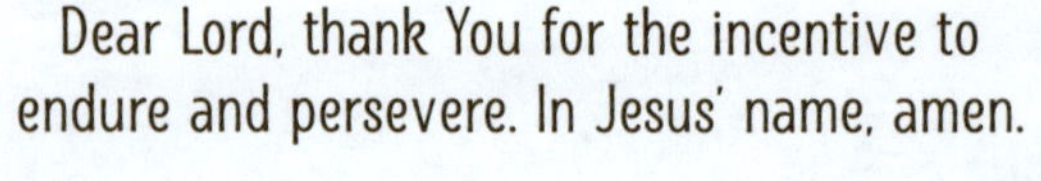

Dear Lord, thank You for the incentive to endure and persevere. In Jesus' name, amen.

THE PROMISE OF CONSISTENCY

My dearly loved brothers and sisters, don't be misled. Every good gift bestowed, every perfect gift received comes to us from above, courtesy of the Father of lights. He is consistent. He won't change His mind or play tricks in the shadows.

JAMES 1:16–17 VOICE

What a blessing to know that God will not change. He simply cannot. We can always count on His promise to be consistent in His will and ways. In a world that constantly changes its mind, knowing the Lord is always reliable can soothe our anxious minds. The heavenly Father doesn't hide or make connecting with Him a challenge. He doesn't play games with our hearts because He knows the stakes are too high. He is a good, good Father.

This means we can trust that every good and perfect gift comes from Him. God is consistently faithful. While it may not always feel this way, He knows what is best and will dependably bestow goodness to those who love Him. We can anchor ourselves to the Lord's promise of steadfast devotion and let it hold us firmly as we weather the world's chaos.

Dear Lord, I'm grateful for Your reliability and desire to love me. Knowing I can place my full trust in You profoundly settles my anxiety. In Jesus' name, amen.

GOD IS NOT SLOW

Now the Lord is not slow about enacting His promise—
slow is how some people want to characterize it—no,
He is not slow but patient and merciful to you, not wanting
anyone to be destroyed, but wanting everyone to turn away
from following his own path and to turn toward God's.
2 PETER 3:9 VOICE

Sometimes God's timing seems slow to us. We may think this reveals apathy or an unwillingness to fulfill His promises. He seems unhurried, not only as we wait for prayers to be answered but also in His return for the church. Is He too busy to help, or are bigger world problems requiring His full attention? With the world being so deeply divided and lines being drawn in the sand, is the Lord tarrying for a good reason? The answer is yes.

The reality is that God isn't slow but patient. God's heart desires that everyone turn away from sin and toward Him. He wants as many as possible to secure their eternity in heaven. That includes those who've not yet seen their need for a Savior and future generations. He's in no rush because His timing is always perfect, even if it's not on our timetable.

Dear Lord, I trust in Your timing for all things. In Jesus' name, amen.

THE PROMISE OF FAVOR

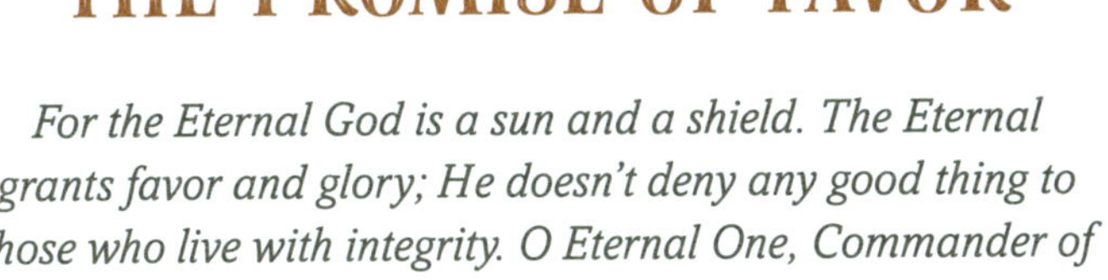

For the Eternal God is a sun and a shield. The Eternal grants favor and glory; He doesn't deny any good thing to those who live with integrity. O Eternal One, Commander of heaven's armies, how fortunate are those who trust You.

Psalm 84:11–12 voice

There are good reasons to pursue righteous living. As believers, it's our great honor to live in ways that delight God's heart. We should want to follow His commands in every area of our lives. Choosing faith over our flesh is difficult, but the Lord will empower us to do just that.

Be kind when you'd rather be right. Extend grace when you'd rather hold a grudge. Be generous when you'd rather turn away. Show compassion when you'd rather pass judgment. Choose self-control when you'd rather indulge. Be thoughtful when you'd rather be selfish. Ask God to strengthen you to live with integrity in a world that tempts you to live only for yourself.

Let the promise in today's verses encourage you to follow His plan. If you make choices that align with His will, you will receive favor. When you walk in the Lord's ways, His goodness follows.

Dear Lord, I want my life to glorify Your name above all else. Help me follow You in pleasing ways. In Jesus' name, amen.

THE PROMISE TO LEAD

Then Moses called for Joshua and said to him, as all Israel watched, "Be strong! Be courageous! For you shall lead these people into the land promised by the Lord to their ancestors; see to it that they conquer it. Don't be afraid, for the Lord will go before you and will be with you; he will not fail nor forsake you."

DEUTERONOMY 31:7–8 TLB

God didn't free the nation of Israel from Egyptian bondage to then let them wander aimlessly in the wilderness. He wasn't sitting back and watching them try to devise a plan. Instead, God was deeply invested in their full deliverance into the Promised Land. He stayed with them from start to finish.

Just as God promised to lead the Israelites and be a constant companion to them, He'll do the same for us today. We can be fully confident in the Lord's leadership, trusting He will help us walk according to His plan. We don't have to worry or be fearful, because the Lord is with us every step of the way. Our job is to follow His lead and trust His guidance.

Dear Lord, knowing Your loving promise to lead me every day is a blessing. Help me surrender my will to Yours and follow where You direct me. In Jesus' name, amen.

HIS SPIRIT AND PEACE

"I'm telling you these things while I'm still living with you. The Friend, the Holy Spirit whom the Father will send at my request, will make everything plain to you. He will remind you of all the things I have told you. I'm leaving you well and whole. That's my parting gift to you. Peace. I don't leave you the way you're used to being left—feeling abandoned, bereft. So don't be upset. Don't be distraught."

JOHN 14:25–27 MSG

Jesus promised the presence of the Holy Spirit and the blessing of supernatural peace. These were His parting gifts before He ascended back into heaven, and they are available to us today. These powerful promises are also for every believer who walks the earth until His return to take us home.

The Spirit guides us in righteous living and reminds us of God's goodness vowed for those who love Him. He brings understanding so we know how to live and love according to His perfect plan. As we press into the Holy Spirit and listen for His leading, we will find peace regardless of our chaotic circumstances. We can rest and trust His guidance.

Dear Lord, I'm grateful for Your Spirit and the everlasting peace that it brings. I need them both! In Jesus' name, amen.

LIVING WITH EXPECTATION

"Let not your heart be troubled. You are trusting God, now trust in me. There are many homes up there where my Father lives, and I am going to prepare them for your coming. When everything is ready, then I will come and get you, so that you can always be with me where I am. If this weren't so, I would tell you plainly."

JOHN 14:1–3 TLB

This promise is one we can take to heart. It's what keeps us going when life feels difficult, settles our spirits when things look hopeless, and keeps us moving forward when we want to give up. It is what we cry out for and are most excited about. Knowing that Jesus has promised to return at His perfect and appointed time and get us out of this dark and discouraging world brings much-needed peace. Eternity in heaven with God is what we long for the very most.

How does this truth help you navigate the ups and downs of life? How does it calm your anxious heart and offer a fresh perspective? Let it encourage you to live today with expectation for heaven. Our hearts may be troubled, but understanding this promise will help quiet our fears.

Dear Lord, help me live with eternal expectation! In Jesus' name, amen.

ASKING FOR WHAT GLORIFIES

Whatever you ask for in My name, I will do it so that the Father will get glory from the Son. Let Me say it again: if you ask for anything in My name, I will do it.

JOHN 14:13–14 VOICE

Let's keep the right perspective regarding this verse. Jesus isn't saying that He'll grant us every worldly and fleshly desire. If we're craving what is ungodly, we won't get it from Him. If we're longing for unhealthy things, God won't provide them. We can't ask for what goes against who He is or what leads us into trouble. The Lord loves us too much for that. But when we are serious about our faith and growing our relationship with Him, our desires change.

God promises that when we ask for what will glorify His name, we will receive it. We can pray for patience in parenting or mercy in marriage. We can request wisdom for work and discernment for decisions. We may need self-control, peace, joy, or the ability to forgive. Our hearts may need rest and our spirits a revival. We can ask for restoration or the willingness to repent. These requests will delight the Lord and He will provide them.

Dear Lord, let my requests grow my faith and bring You glory! In Jesus' name, amen.

OUTDOING EACH OTHER

Now we can look forward to the salvation God has promised us. There is no longer any room for doubt, and we can tell others that salvation is ours, for there is no question that he will do what he says. In response to all he has done for us, let us outdo each other in being helpful and kind to each other and in doing good.

Hebrews 10:23–24 TLB

The writer of Hebrews makes an excellent suggestion for believers. God's Word is solid, and He's a keeper of every promise—so in response, we should outdo one another in meaningful ways. God's goodness is so wonderful that it should prompt us to live with abundant kindness and generosity toward others. We should desire to do good for them. Out of the fullness of our hearts, compassion should flow in greater measure to bless people we encounter.

What has God done for you? How have you experienced His goodness? How has He healed or restored you? How has He brought you comfort and rest? How has He opened or closed appropriate doors? Let His goodness encourage you to extend the same grace to others.

Dear Lord, let Your goodness in my life prompt me to show goodness to those around me. In Jesus' name, amen.

GIVING BURDENS TO GOD

Give your burdens to the Lord. He will carry them.
He will not permit the godly to slip or fall.
Psalm 55:22 TLB

Why do we try so hard to carry our own burdens? Our best efforts are no match to God's knowledge and might. We're weak in comparison, often ineffective, and always flawed. We see only part of the issue, while He can see it in its entirety from beginning to end. He knows the complexity of how we got tangled up and the right way to remove the knots. He promises to faithfully intervene and carry the burdens weighing us down so we don't have to. God wants you to leave every heartache, worry, and fear at His feet.

It can be challenging to let go and trust the Lord. Maybe you're afraid of being judged or are struggling with pride and don't want to admit you need help. Maybe you're ashamed to be tangled in the same mess yet again or are too stubborn to surrender yourself to His most capable hands.

Don't let anything dampen your faith or your ability to trust God. No matter how you feel, He loves you and wants to take burdens off your shoulders and replace them with His peace.

Dear Lord, I give my burdens to You. In Jesus' name, amen.

STAYING THE COURSE

"The one who conquers through faithfulness even unto death will be clothed in white garments, and I will certainly not erase that person's name from the book of life. I will acknowledge this person's name before My Father and before His heavenly messengers."

REVELATION 3:5 VOICE

In this letter to the church in Sardis, John writes to them as instructed by Jesus. They had a reputation for being alive as a church, but they were spiritually dead instead. The pews were filled with unbelievers just going through the motions. But some were faithful, and He tried to affirm and encourage them to stay the course because they weren't soiled by sin.

Revelation 3:5 promises that the one who conquers is born again and that their name is secured in eternity in the book of life. They will be acknowledged by Jesus in heaven. As believers, this same promise is guaranteed to us too. Like the faithful in Sardis, be encouraged to stay the course and pursue righteous living. It's not about being perfect but choosing to live each day with intentionality.

Dear Lord, I want You to see my efforts to glorify Your name in how I navigate the ups and downs of this life. Help me make the right choices. In Jesus' name, amen.

THE POWER OF GOD'S WORD

Let the words from the book of the law be always on your lips. Meditate on them day and night so that you may be careful to live by all that is written in it. If you do, as you make your way through this world, you will prosper and always find success.

JOSHUA 1:8 VOICE

Knowing God's Word and putting it into action sets us up for good things. It will help us find success in living a holy life that delights the Lord. Our faith will grow, our resolve will strengthen, and we'll live with the hope of Jesus. These are promises! So how do we effectively invest in His Word to reap the blessings?

It is well worth your time to dig into scripture daily. Read the verses, think about them, and imagine how to put what you've read into action. Mark up your Bible, underlining and making notes. Talk to God and ask Him to help you faithfully follow His commands. Be honest about what feels too hard or where you're afraid of failing. Ask questions, looking for clarification. Check out trusted commentaries or study notes for the Bible. Let God's Word sink into your heart through purposeful study and meditation.

Dear Lord, I love Your Word! In Jesus' name, amen.

THE PROMISE TO REMAIN

This is My command: be strong and courageous. Never be afraid or discouraged because I am your God, the Eternal One, and I will remain with you wherever you go.

JOSHUA 1:9 VOICE

The Lord commanded Joshua to be strong and courageous, saying obedience was possible because of His promised presence. That's a bold statement, but it's true. God gives us *everything* needed to do hard things. God promised to remain with Joshua no matter what, and we have that same pledge from the Lord today.

Knowing He is close should supernaturally calm any anxiety we're facing. When worried, it should blanket us with comfort. Fear may try to sneak in and steal our peace, but turning our thoughts to God and His goodness will miraculously settle our spirit. His nearness has the power to strengthen believers to do the impossible.

Are you anxious about a hard conversation, stressed over a weighty decision, or fearful of how someone will respond to you putting healthy boundaries in place? Are your finances freaking you out, or is a medical condition causing sleepless nights? You can relax in the promise that God is with you wherever you go.

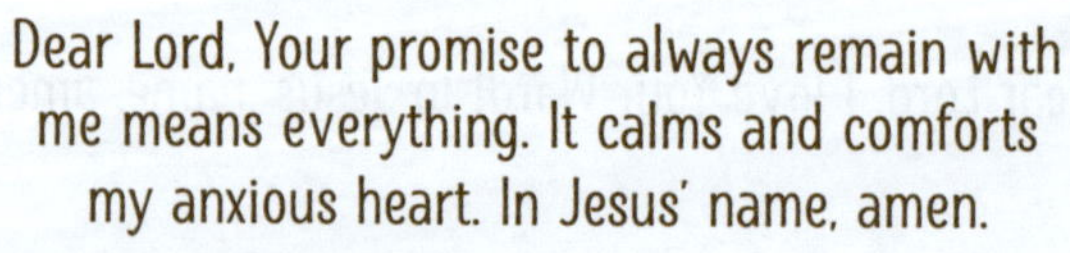

Dear Lord, Your promise to always remain with me means everything. It calms and comforts my anxious heart. In Jesus' name, amen.

GOOD AND GODLY FRIENDSHIPS

Don't be teamed with those who do not love the Lord, for what do the people of God have in common with the people of sin? How can light live with darkness? . . . That is why the Lord has said, "Leave them; separate yourselves from them; don't touch their filthy things, and I will welcome you and be a Father to you, and you will be my sons and daughters."

2 CORINTHIANS 6:14, 17–18 TLB

This isn't about having an elitist attitude or thinking we're better than others. It's not about segregating ourselves because of a critical heart. This is a reminder that we are who we hang out with. That's why being surrounded by a godly community that loves the Lord and points us to Him is important. We should never be rude or condescending to unbelievers, nor should we saturate ourselves in their lifestyles or attitudes.

When we invest in good and godly friendships and pursue a righteous life that pleases God, He promises His presence. Because we have accepted Jesus as our Savior, we are His daughters. He will welcome us into the family. Until we see Him in heaven, it's vital we keep company with those who will encourage us in our faith.

Dear Lord, help me keep good and godly company. In Jesus' name, amen.

TEMPTATIONS

But remember this—the wrong desires that come into your life aren't anything new and different. Many others have faced exactly the same problems before you. And no temptation is irresistible. You can trust God to keep the temptation from becoming so strong that you can't stand up against it, for he has promised this and will do what he says. He will show you how to escape temptation's power so that you can bear up patiently against it.

1 CORINTHIANS 10:13 TLB

In this life, we'll face temptations regularly. We'll be tempted to say hurtful things in the heat of the moment. We may be lured into bad behavior online—from talking to an old flame to coveting others' stuff to getting in arguments on social media. Instead of being honest, we might tweak the truth for our benefit. Our hearts may be filled with judgment, making us treat others with disdain and disrespect. But there's hope! God promises that with His help, these temptations are manageable.

The enemy specializes in enticing believers into disobedience. But we don't have to fall prey because the Lord will keep every temptation from becoming so strong that we can't overcome it. As we pray, He'll show us how to escape its clutches.

Dear Lord, thank You for providing
a way out. In Jesus' name, amen.

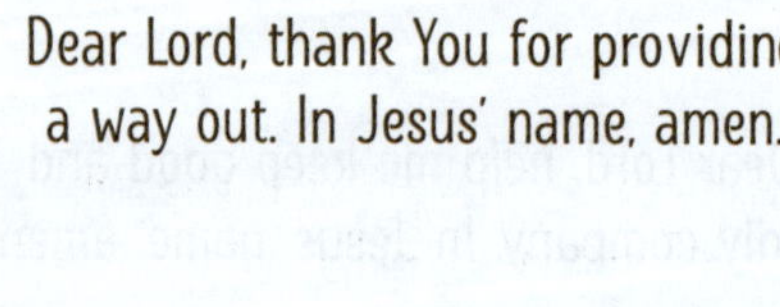

THOSE WORN, HARD PATHS

He provides me rest in rich, green fields beside streams of refreshing water. He soothes my fears; He makes me whole again, steering me off worn, hard paths to roads where truth and righteousness echo His name.

PSALM 23:2–3 VOICE

You might be walking some worn, hard paths today. Maybe your adult children are acting in hurtful ways to your new spouse, or you're feeling beaten down by a long divorce battle. You may be overwhelmed with grief after losing someone you loved deeply. Did a treatment plan fall short of hopeful expectations? Are you worried you'll never find a husband? Are you struggling to get pregnant? Are you unable to find that much-needed job? Cry out to God, because He is listening.

Rather than try to traverse this rocky path alone, remember that according to today's verse, the heavenly Father promises to bring comfort to the weary. He will restore your soul and give you a renewing rest, making you whole again. You'll find peace in the chaos and be invigorated by His presence as you press in. You may try to fix yourself with grit and worldly remedies, but this is something only God can do.

Dear Lord, I trust You to help me find my footing on the right path. In Jesus' name, amen.

YOUR NAVIGATION GUIDE

Even in the unending shadows of death's darkness, I am not overcome by fear. Because You are with me in those dark moments, near with Your protection and guidance, I am comforted.

PSALM 23:4 VOICE

Part of the human experience is navigating life's difficulties. We have mountaintop moments where everything feels joyous, and then there are times when we're deep in the valley, overwhelmed by sadness and fear. This is normal and to be expected by everyone who lives and breathes on planet earth. But believers have an edge over those who don't trust in the Lord. We have a hope that offers an unmatched sense of comfort, even in the darkest times. It's the Lord's presence.

Can you recall getting bad news but feeling strength instead of despair, or being in a challenging conversation and feeling peaceful rather than defensive? Have you remained calm and positive even when your finances were underwater, or have you felt God's divine perspective of your worthiness shine through even when you've been rejected by someone? It's because of His promises to always be with you in those dark moments to protect, guide, and comfort.

Dear Lord, what a relief to know You will never leave me to navigate the valleys of life alone. In Jesus' name, amen.

THE GOD OF PROVISION

You spread out a table before me, provisions in the midst of attack from my enemies; You care for all my needs, anointing my head with soothing, fragrant oil, filling my cup again and again with Your grace. Certainly Your faithful protection and loving provision will pursue me where I go, always, everywhere. I will always be with the Eternal, in Your house forever.

Psalm 23:5–6 voice

David, a man after God's own heart, is the author of the twenty-third Psalm. When he mentions that the Lord has spread out a table before him, it likens to Paul telling the church in Philippi that He will meet all their needs according to His glorious riches (Philippians 4:19). Just like David and Paul, believers today serve a God who promises to provide for those who love Him. We can be confident of this promise because He is faithful and unchanging.

Yes, the Lord knows your needs, and He will care for them—*every single one*. His grace is endless, and your cup of it will always be replenished. As His beloved, God promises to protect you wherever you go while here and promises eternity with Him in heaven.

Dear Lord, You are all I need. In Jesus' name, amen.

WATCHING GOD WORK

Moses spoke to the people: "Don't be afraid. Stand firm and watch God do his work of salvation for you today. Take a good look at the Egyptians today for you're never going to see them again. God will fight the battle for you. And you? You keep your mouths shut!"

EXODUS 14:13–14 MSG

Sometimes, the best thing we can do is keep our mouths shut and watch God work. Rather than get tangled in fear and repeatedly process it with our friends and family, what if we stood firm in our faith and trusted His plan? He has promised to play an integral part in our lives as provider and protector. The Lord will give us safe passage through our struggles. While there are times when we must fight battles in His strength, there are also times when we must stand firm in our faith and watch as He fights for us.

Moses spoke the words in today's verses to the Israelites at the foot of the Red Sea. They had Pharaoh and his army on one side and a huge body of water on the other. They were trapped and needed God to intervene. He made a way for them, and He will make a way for you too.

Dear Lord, I'm watching. In Jesus' name, amen.

PROMISES COME TO PASS

That day the Eternal rescued Israel from the powerful grip of the Egyptians, and Israel watched the corpses of the Egyptians wash up on the shore. When Israel witnessed the incredible power that the Eternal used to defeat the Egyptians, the people were struck with fear of Him, and they trusted in Him and also in Moses, His servant.

EXODUS 14:30–31 VOICE

God is faithful to keep His word. When He told the Israelites, through Moses, that they'd never see the Egyptians again, it happened. They safely passed through the Red Sea on dry ground, and the force of Pharaoh's army didn't. The waters closed in on them and they died. They were reduced to corpses.

Seeing God's promise come to pass deeply affected their hearts. They were awestruck by His awesomeness, which gave them confidence to trust in their deliverance and their deliverer.

The same reality applies to us today, which is why we should document the times God's promises occur in our lives. We need that reminder to trust in Him again, especially when our circumstances look hopeless.

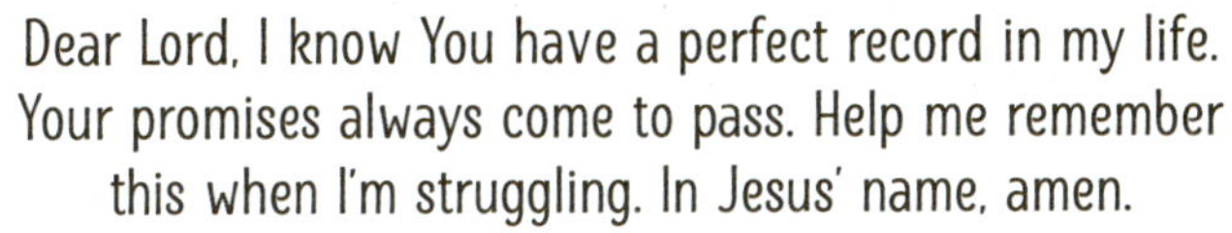

Dear Lord, I know You have a perfect record in my life. Your promises always come to pass. Help me remember this when I'm struggling. In Jesus' name, amen.

NOT ALLOWED

I have created the blacksmith who readies the fire and forges weapons for wars; And I have created the destroyer to ravage and ruin. But no instrument forged against you will be allowed to hurt you, and no voice raised to condemn you will successfully prosecute you. It's that simple; this is how it will be for the servants of the Eternal; I will vindicate them.

ISAIAH 54:16–17 VOICE

When the prophet Isaiah relayed God's future promise to the Israelites about the restoration of Jerusalem, he said no instrument forged would be allowed to hurt them. How does He know this for sure? It's because He created the one who makes the weapons. God can make them effective or unproductive. In all things and in all ways, He is in charge.

That truth is still active for us today. As the enemy comes after us, working to destroy our peace and joy, we can hold on to this promise as well. He may wreak havoc, and we may feel crushed by our circumstances—but ultimately, the devil's tactics will fail.

Dear Lord, sometimes I'm overwhelmed by the evil coming my way. It feels too big and too much. Thank You for being in charge and promising to protect and deliver me. In Jesus' name, amen.

IRREVOCABLE

Just as in the time of Noah I swore that I would never again permit the waters of a flood to cover the earth and destroy its life, so now I swear that I will never again pour out my anger on you. For the mountains may depart and the hills disappear, but my kindness shall not leave you. My promise of peace for you will never be broken, says the Lord who has mercy upon you.

Isaiah 54:9–10 TLB

We can breathe a big sigh of relief knowing God won't pour out His anger on believers. We'll be delivered from His wrath of that magnitude. This doesn't mean we won't face challenging times and moments where we feel overwhelmed. Things may continue to be rough in our families, communities, states, nation, and world, but we can rest assured that God's kindness will be our constant companion. Peace will be available for those who seek it daily. His mercy will always be evident.

Until we see Jesus face-to-face, let's celebrate God's faithfulness and powerful promises to those who love Him. We don't have to live in fear or worry that our mistakes will result in disqualification from His vows.

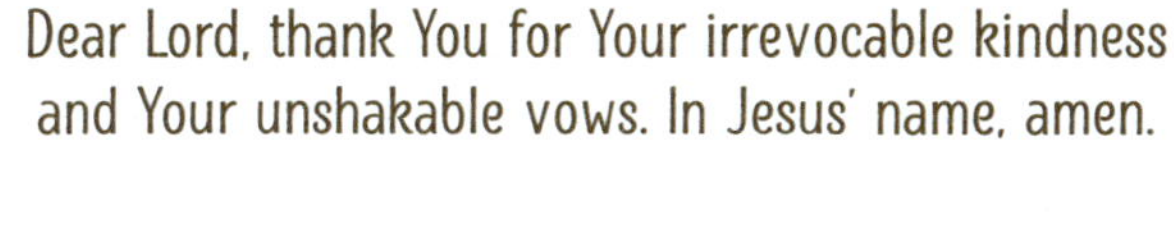

Dear Lord, thank You for Your irrevocable kindness and Your unshakable vows. In Jesus' name, amen.

KEEPING GOD'S COMPANY

"Are you tired? Worn out? Burned out on religion? Come to me. Get away with me and you'll recover your life. I'll show you how to take a real rest. Walk with me and work with me—watch how I do it. Learn the unforced rhythms of grace. I won't lay anything heavy or ill-fitting on you. Keep company with me and you'll learn to live freely and lightly."

MATTHEW 11:28–30 MSG

When life beats us down, God invites us to seek Him. He promises to bring restoration. He is the safest place we can go when we're feeling overwhelmed. Every hopeless feeling is met with God's goodness. Our struggles will be silenced with peace as we embrace His divine perspective. We'll find rest in His presence as we lay down our worries and burdens. Our spirits will be settled from the relentless stress that keeps us stirred up. Each fearful thought will melt away by His grace.

Keep God's company and discover what true freedom feels like. He promises to meet you in every messy moment and bring the comfort you need.

Dear Lord, I'm so grateful that You love me no matter how difficult my life seems. You're there for me in every situation. I will keep Your company and receive Your promised goodness. In Jesus' name, amen.

HE STRENGTHENS THE WEARY

Don't you know? Haven't you heard? The Eternal, the Everlasting God, The Creator of the whole world, never gets tired or weary. His wisdom is beyond understanding. God strengthens the weary and gives vitality to those worn down by age and care.

Isaiah 40:28–29 voice

Life's worries and frustrations may make us grow weary, but they don't do that to God. We may feel emotionally and physically exhausted by all we must navigate during the day with family and work, but He is never overwhelmed. When we're out of innovative ideas on how to handle the ups and downs of life, God always sees the right path forward. Why? Because He isn't hindered by the human condition. He has endless energy, steadfast strength, limitless love, and never-ending knowledge.

Let this encourage you today! You don't have to be a superhero. You don't have to wear yourself out. Ask God for help. He knows when you fall short and promises to make up the difference. You will receive the get-up-and-go you need when you need it.

Dear Lord, I confess that I often try to get through each day with my own strength. Thank You for promising to meet me there and revitalizing me in abundance. In Jesus' name, amen.

HIS PEACE WILL REIGN

You will keep the peace, a perfect peace, for all who trust in You, for those who dedicate their hearts and minds to You. So trust in the Eternal One forever, for He is like a great Rock—strong, stable, trustworthy, and lasting.
ISAIAH 26:3–4 VOICE

More than anything else, we need God's supernatural peace to help us navigate the difficulties of this world. We need Him to calm our anxious thoughts and settle our fearful hearts. There's just so much to worry about. From the struggles in parenting to the challenges of infertility. From wrestling with marriage woes to grappling with singlehood. From money issues to health scares. We hear of wars and rumors of wars, civil unrest in our communities, and tensions within families. The world is a hot mess, full of chaos and confusion. We need the Lord's peace to reign in us daily.

God promises that when we trust Him and commit ourselves to holy and pleasing lives, His peace will govern our hearts and minds. With His help, we can do it. The Lord will equip us for righteous living, and our obedience will result in a needed sense of peace.

Dear Lord, my heart is troubled by many things, and I need Your peace to reign in me. In Jesus' name, amen.

A FUTURE PROMISE

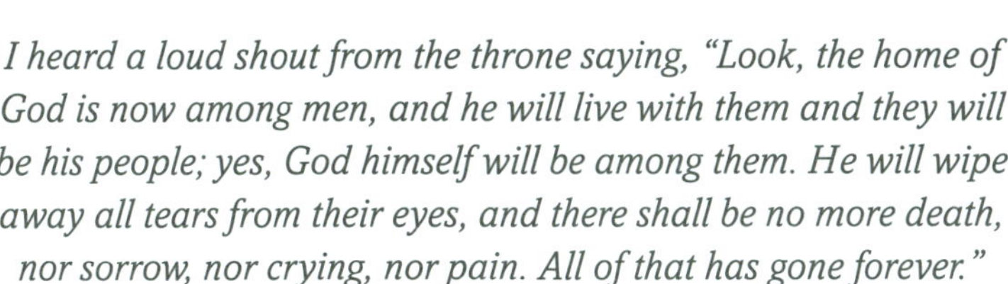

I heard a loud shout from the throne saying, "Look, the home of God is now among men, and he will live with them and they will be his people; yes, God himself will be among them. He will wipe away all tears from their eyes, and there shall be no more death, nor sorrow, nor crying, nor pain. All of that has gone forever."

REVELATION 21:3–4 TLB

In a vision, John saw the holy city, the new Jerusalem, coming down from heaven. Of course, this is a future promise that has not yet come to pass. Believers can look forward to it, especially knowing that God Himself will be among us. We experience His presence now, but one can only imagine what it will be like to have the Lord that close to us daily.

Another promise we can rely on is knowing there will be no tears in heaven. Why? Because it will be void of anything that might bring them forth. Living here and feeling such pain and suffering makes it challenging to imagine a place without them. Yet we're assured heaven is such a place, and we can look forward to eternity there.

Dear Lord, I'm excited that my forever home will be nothing like my temporary one. In Jesus' name, amen.

ETERNAL LIFE FOR BELIEVING

Jesus told her, "I am the one who raises the dead and gives them life again. Anyone who believes in me, even though he dies like anyone else, shall live again. He is given eternal life for believing in me and shall never perish. Do you believe this, Martha?" "Yes, Master," she told him. "I believe you are the Messiah, the Son of God, the one we have so long awaited."

JOHN 11:25–27 TLB

Martha's faith is notable. Rather than doubt or ask for continuous proof, she decided to believe Jesus was who He said He was. She didn't let doubt creep in and keep her stuck in unbelief. This bold choice secured her eternity in heaven with God. Her faith was unshakable.

This same belief is how we secure our heavenly home. By trusting Jesus' words, we're promised a future forever with Him. Nothing can steal it away from us. We can't lose it because of our bad choices or seasons of sinning, and disobedience won't make it invalid. We can't exhaust God and make Him turn away from us because of our imperfections. Instead, we can be confident that our salvation is promised to be a lasting covenant with God.

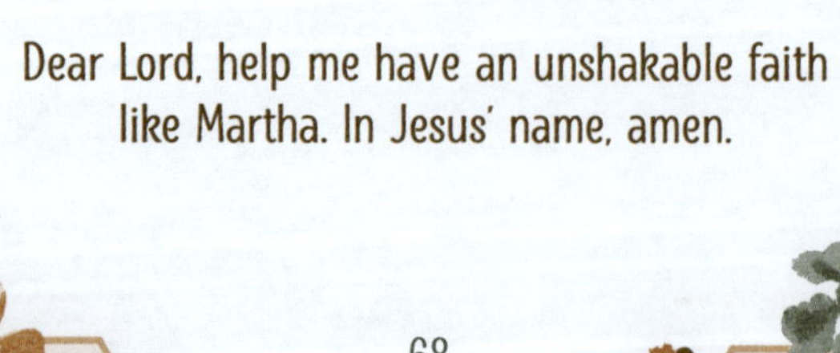

Dear Lord, help me have an unshakable faith like Martha. In Jesus' name, amen.

YOUR OBEDIENCE IS BLESSED

If I close up the heavens and their rain and send any of the disasters you described—drought, locusts, pestilence—to ravish the land and people; and My people (who are known by My name) humbly pray, follow My commandments, and abandon any actions or thoughts that might lead to further sinning, then I shall hear their prayers from My house in heaven, I shall forgive their sins, and I shall save their land from the disasters.

2 CHRONICLES 7:13–14 VOICE

God blesses obedience. This truth is confirmed not only in today's verse but also throughout the Bible. Proverbs 8:32 says, "So now listen to me, my children: those who live by my ways will find true happiness." Luke 11:28 says, "How blessed are those who hear God's voice and make God's message their way of life." And Psalm 106:3 says, "Blessed are those who work for justice, who always do what they know to be right!"

Let's be women who know and follow God's commands, even when we don't get it perfect. Let's be prayerful and humble, intentionally pursuing living in ways that glorify His name. He is ready to bless our obedience!

Dear Lord, empower me to follow Your will and ways every day. In Jesus' name, amen.

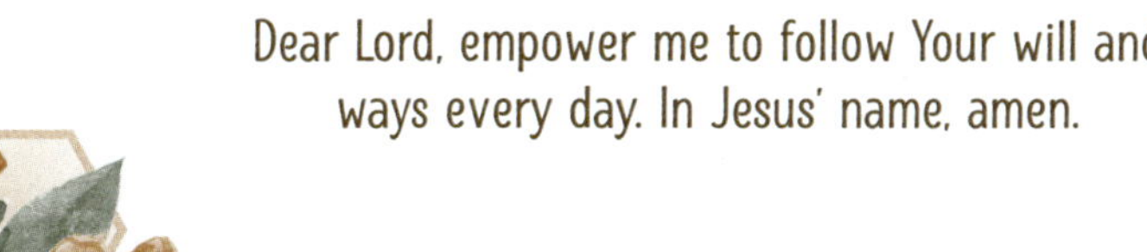

FOLLOWING HIS WAYS

If you follow My ways as your father David did, do all that I ask you to do, and follow My laws and commands, then I will establish your royal throne and keep My covenant with your father David: "One of your descendants will always be a king of Israel." If you and the Israelites ignore My ways and disregard My laws, if you serve other gods and worship them, then I will remove you all from My land.

2 Chronicles 7:17–20 VOICE

What's God asking of you? Is He asking you to trust Him in the middle of a messy season of marriage or to forgive someone who has deeply hurt your feelings? Is the Lord asking you to let go of control and let Him take the wheel? Are you being asked to show compassion when it feels impossible? Is God asking you to trust Him with your health, finances, or career decisions? Is He asking you to choose faith over your fleshly desires in more ways than one? For as long as we breathe on planet earth, we'll navigate the tension between God's will and our own. The promise is that He'll see our obedience and reward those hard-won decisions.

Dear Lord, I want to live like You want me to.
Help me obey. In Jesus' name, amen.

ABIDING

I am the vine, and you are the branches. If you abide in Me and I in you, you will bear great fruit. Without Me, you will accomplish nothing. If anyone does not abide in Me, he is like a branch that is tossed out and shrivels up and is later gathered to be tossed into the fire to burn.

JOHN 15:5–6 VOICE

Simply put, when we stay close to God—abide in Him—our faith will be evident in the words we say and the actions we take. We will bear great fruit because we'll be connected to our source for all things. He empowers us to live righteously, enabling believers to follow His commands passionately and purposefully. Our steadfast faith allows us to love the unlovable and forgive the unforgivable. It inspires us to be His hands and feet to a lost and broken world. We're emboldened to be kind and generous with our time, talent, and treasure according to His plan for our lives. Without that vital connection, our pursuit of a right relationship with God will shrivel up.

His promise to you is that when you stay connected, you'll find abundance in Him. You'll be able to live and love in miraculous and supernatural ways.

Dear Lord, You are my source. In Jesus' name, amen.

THE PROMISE OF THE SPIRIT

I will send a great Helper to you from the Father, one known as the Spirit of truth. He comes from the Father and will point to the truth as it concerns Me. But you will also point others to the truth about My identity, because you have journeyed with Me since this all began.

JOHN 15:26–27 VOICE

Jesus promised the gift of the Holy Spirit to His disciples and later to those who accepted Him as their Savior. As our helper, the Spirit enables us to understand God's will and how we are meant to walk it out. He activates our faith and guides us in it. Sometimes it's a gut feeling that leads us to make a certain decision. It may be a clear directive to choose one specific path over another one. Or it may be keen discernment that cuts through the confusion of a situation. Regardless, the Holy Spirit helps us make faith-filled decisions so we can live righteously and please the Lord.

This is one of God's sweetest promises. The moment we are born again, the Spirit takes up residency in our hearts, and He will never leave.

Dear Lord, thank You for the gift of the Holy Spirit and His constant companionship. In Jesus' name, amen.

PROMISE OF FREEDOM

Jesus replied, "You are slaves of sin, every one of you. And slaves don't have rights, but the Son has every right there is! So if the Son sets you free, you will indeed be free."

JOHN 8:34–36 TLB

Jesus came to the world with a powerful purpose. It was His death on the cross that brought us everlasting freedom from sin. We were dead in those transgressions—enslaved by them—and Jesus paid the ransom, so they were no longer able to keep us in bondage. He promised to set us free, and the Lord keeps His word.

Have you thanked God for His goodness lately? Have you told Him how much you appreciate how He set you free from sin? When was the last time you prayed with a heart of thanksgiving, recognizing His kindness and generous spirit? Why not make time right now to reveal your gratitude? There's no better time than this moment to say thank you. As a believer, your eternity is secure in heaven because Jesus intervened on your behalf.

Dear Lord, I am humbled that You sent Your one and only Son to pay for my sins—past, present, and future. Thank You for the promise of freedom. In Jesus' name, amen.

HE HOLDS YOUR HAND

After all, it is I, the Eternal One your God,
who has hold of your right hand, who whispers in
your ear, "Don't be afraid. I will help you."
ISAIAH 41:13 VOICE

This promise melts our hearts and brings much-needed comfort to our weary souls, especially when we're battling fear. It settles us when we can't stop worrying and comforts us when we're stressed out. To know that God is close enough to hold our hand—that He even wants to connect with us in such a way—is a priceless feeling. This promise to help us when life feels too big or out of control is unmatched by anything the world can offer.

When you're stressed, where do you find relief? Maybe you overeat, lose yourself in a novel, or hide under the covers and sleep. You might relax by scrolling through social media or watching hour after hour of movies. You may find solace in a conversation with your best friend or time spent with your family. While all of these can bring comfort, they are temporary. But God's promise to be with you lasts forever.

Dear Lord, I'm struggling. Please draw close to me now and bring me comfort. In Jesus' name, amen.

A SAVING FAITH

So if you believe deep in your heart that God raised Jesus from the pit of death and if you voice your allegiance by confessing the truth that "Jesus is Lord," then you will be saved! Belief begins in the heart and leads to a life that's right with God; confession departs from our lips and brings eternal salvation.

Romans 10:9–10 VOICE

The promise of salvation comes from believing that Jesus died on the cross and rose again three days later and confessing that Jesus is Lord. Don't let this belief and declaration be only head knowledge. Instead, make certain they sink deep into your heart and become real and true to you.

James 2:19 says, "Do you think that just believing there's one God is going to get you anywhere? The demons believe that too, and it terrifies them!" Without a genuine belief from the heart, one may not actually have a saving faith. For those who do, God's promise is clear. We will have eternal salvation and experience His presence in person forever!

Dear Lord, I believe in my heart that You died and rose again and are now my Savior. I know I have a saving faith and will spend eternity with You. In Jesus' name, amen.

HIS WORD IS UNSHAKEN

The Eternal didn't become devoted to you and choose you because you were the most numerous of all the peoples—in fact, you were the least! Instead, He brought you out of Egypt with overwhelming power and liberated you from slavery to Pharaoh the king because He loved you and was keeping the oath He swore to your ancestors.

DEUTERONOMY 7:7–8 VOICE

There is nobody who has better follow-through than the Lord. Once a promise is made, that promise is kept. Today's verses drive that point home with clarity.

God was deliberate in choosing the nation of Israel to be the lineage for His Son's entrance into the world. They were to spread the gospel message, be missionaries, and minister to the world. They were specifically chosen to point others to God, something they often messed up spectacularly. But the promises He made to that nation were unencumbered by their unfaithfulness and failings. His love endured their shortcomings.

The same is true for us today. We have the same assurances that God's promises to us will be realized. Even when we make mistakes and don't follow through, His word is unshaken.

Dear Lord, what a relief to know Your promises aren't based on our perfection. In Jesus' name, amen.

EFFECTIVE AND HOLY LIVING

Since everything here today might well be gone tomorrow, do you see how essential it is to live a holy life? Daily expect the Day of God, eager for its arrival. The galaxies will burn up and the elements melt down that day—but we'll hardly notice. We'll be looking the other way, ready for the promised new heavens and the promised new earth, all landscaped with righteousness.

2 PETER 3:11–13 MSG

Peter encourages us to live effective and holy lives until Jesus' return. Knowing the Lord is coming back should motivate us to live a righteous lifestyle. Our focus should be on eternal things rather than earthly ones because we cannot take anything with us. We should live with hope and anticipation, readying ourselves to see the Lord and the promised new heavens and earth.

What does that look like? How do we live with an expectant heart? Spend time in the Word daily, learning about God and what righteous living looks like. Deepen your relationship with Him through continual prayer. Look for opportunities to bless those around you, sharing your testimony at the right times and in the right ways.

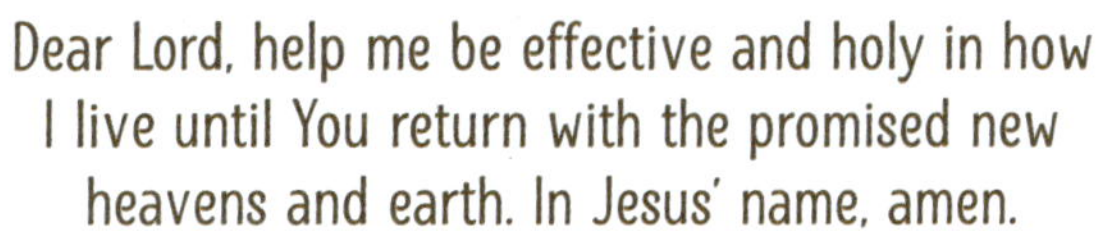

Dear Lord, help me be effective and holy in how I live until You return with the promised new heavens and earth. In Jesus' name, amen.

ASK, SEEK, KNOCK

Just ask and it will be given to you; seek after it and you will find. Continue to knock and the door will be opened for you. All who ask receive. Those who seek, find what they seek. And he who knocks, will have the door opened.

MATTHEW 7:7–8 VOICE

Our God is accessible. He doesn't hide or put us through the wringer before we can connect with Him. He won't keep His goodness at bay, and He doesn't find pleasure in stringing us along. God is never too busy to listen and respond when we pray. Instead, we're told to ask, seek, and knock.

We are encouraged to ask for what we need in prayer, trusting He will answer with what is best for us, even if it's not necessarily what we request. We are instructed to seek God's presence continually and wholeheartedly, paying attention with confident expectation. We're advised to knock with persistence, purpose, and passion until our plea is answered.

As you take these verses to heart, commit to pursuing God verbally, in your thoughts, and with your actions. He promises that in return, when we ask, we will receive. When we seek, we will find. And when we knock with determination, the door will be opened.

Dear Lord, thank You for being accessible.
In Jesus' name, amen.

THE GOLDEN RULE

This is what our Scriptures come to teach: in everything, in every circumstance, do to others as you would have them do to you.

MATTHEW 7:12 VOICE

This verse from the Sermon on the Mount is often referred to as the Golden Rule. It's a powerful way for believers to gauge how they are treating others. When we walk this out with purpose, it pleases the Lord. How do we know that? Matthew 22:39 reveals His second greatest commandment, which is to love our neighbors as ourselves. That's what we'd be doing. The Bible is full of reminders that God promises to bless our obedience.

Think back to the past few days. Maybe you're holding a grudge and have spoken unkindly to someone, or maybe you're letting your annoyance shine through more than your love. Are you punishing someone by ignoring them and refusing to discuss an issue you're having? Are you being stingy with your time, unwilling to help others? Or have you tried your best to love others, be quick to forgive, have a servant's heart, and lead with kindness and generosity?

Let's be women who delight the Lord with how we treat those around us, both strangers and those we know.

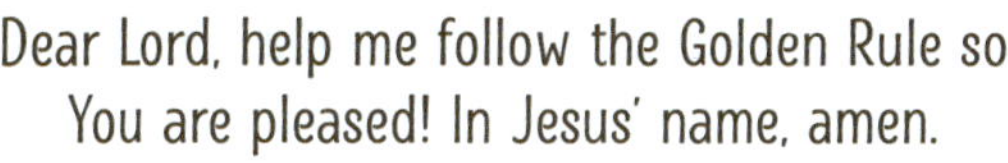

Dear Lord, help me follow the Golden Rule so
You are pleased! In Jesus' name, amen.

PROMISE OF SECURITY

Those people who are listening to Me, those people who hear what I say and live according to My teachings—you are like a wise man who built his house on a rock, on a firm foundation. When storms hit, rain pounded down and waters rose, levies broke and winds beat all the walls of that house. But the house did not fall because it was built upon rock.

MATTHEW 7:24–25 VOICE

When we make the Lord our foundation of faith, nothing this life throws our way will take us out. Our health may fail, our finances may falter, and our careers may come tumbling down into ruin, but we will prevail in victory. Relationships may break apart, our kids may choose the wrong path, and we may experience copious amounts of rejection, but we'll find comfort in God. Why? Because we built our faith on the rock.

Jesus promised that when we do, we will find strength to withstand every storm. While the enemy might unleash his best efforts to bring us down, it won't work. We may get hit on every side and in every way, but God will keep His promise to keep us sturdy and secure.

Dear Lord, help me build my faith
in You alone! In Jesus' name, amen.

GOD'S UNSHAKABLE PRESENCE

Keep your lives free from the love of money, and be content with what you have because He has said, "I will never leave you; I will always be by your side." Because of this promise, we may boldly say, The Lord is my help— I won't be afraid of anything. How can anyone harm me?

HEBREWS 13:5–6 VOICE

While money itself isn't a problem, the love of money is disruptive to the heart of a believer. When we crave money, it becomes an obsession that drives us to work longer and harder to buy things we don't really need. Our focus turns from righteous living to living at a frantic pace because we think it will save us. We think it will allow us to keep up with others or provide security in an unstable world. It may even buy us an elevated status or the respect we desire.

God promises something even greater: His unshakable presence. He knows that's what we truly need to feel safe and secure in an ever-shifting world. The Lord will settle our spirits from a constant state of striving. He will calm our fear of missing out or falling short. As our hearts are full and content, we will find rest.

Dear Lord, I crave Your presence alone. In Jesus' name, amen.

YOUR HIDING PLACE

You are my hiding place from every storm of life; you even keep me from getting into trouble! You surround me with songs of victory. I will instruct you (says the Lord) and guide you along the best pathway for your life; I will advise you and watch your progress.

Psalm 32:7–8 TLB

When your health is deteriorating, your relationships are crumbling, you've been betrayed, or your plans fall apart, let prayer be your first stop. God is your hiding place when the storms roll in. Let His presence surround you, bringing peace to the chaos.

Too often, we look to the world for help. We binge on comfort food and comfort movies to numb the pain. We hit the stores for some retail therapy to boost our mood. We cry to our girlfriends or call our parents for sympathy. We overuse prescription medication or pour another glass of wine. While we may find relief and comfort for a bit, every worldly remedy eventually falls short.

Why not take the Lord up on His offer? As a believer, you have direct access to the goodness of God and the protection He offers. He will show you the path forward, personally guiding your every step.

Dear Lord, You're my hiding place. In Jesus' name, amen.

TIGHTLY WRAPPED LOVE

Tormented and empty are wicked and destructive people, but the one who trusts in the Eternal is wrapped tightly in His gracious love. Express your joy; be happy in Him, you who are good and true. Go ahead, shout and rejoice aloud, you whose hearts are honest and straightforward.

PSALM 32:10–11 VOICE

Have you ever just needed a giant bear hug? Maybe you got some shocking news, or you felt the sting of rejection, or the weight of grief was too overwhelming. While you may have put on a brave face to those around you, inside you were heartbroken. If so, today's verses are a timely reminder of God's promise to wrap you tightly in His love. You'll feel it press in on every side and hold you close.

When you anchor your trust in the Lord, you'll experience His goodness this way. You will have reason to express joy and be happy in Him. Your rejoicing may be demonstrative as you stay honest and humble, for God's presence has surrounded you and brought comfort. When you need it the most, He will make good on His promise to wrap you up tightly in His love.

Dear Lord, I need Your comfort today. Hold me close and restore my heart. In Jesus' name, amen.

GOD'S FOLLOW-THROUGH

God is not a man—He doesn't lie. God isn't the son of a man to want to take back what He's said, or say something and not follow through, or speak and not act on it.

NUMBERS 23:19 VOICE

God's promises are not just empty words on a page but a reality of what believers can expect. Every promise God has made will come to fruition. Each divine vow will be realized. You can trust that the Lord will follow through. He will act on them. Not one promise will be taken back. God doesn't lie, so we can be confident in His words.

What are some of these powerful promises? He will protect His children (Psalm 121). His love will never fail (1 Chronicles 16:34). He will comfort us in our trials (2 Corinthians 1:3–4). God will work all things for good (Romans 8:28). We will find peace when we pray (Philippians 4:6–7). He will meet our needs (Matthew 6:33). Believers will find abundant life (John 10:10). Eternal life is guaranteed for those who trust in Him (John 4:14). And Jesus will return for us (John 14:2–3). We can cling to every promise with assurance and conviction.

Dear Lord, You are a God of Your word. I will trust in Your promises. In Jesus' name, amen.

GOD'S HEFTY PROMISE

"The Father loves this man because he is his Son, and God has given him everything there is. And all who trust him—God's Son—to save them have eternal life; those who don't believe and obey him shall never see heaven, but the wrath of God remains upon them."

JOHN 3:35–36 TLB

God has made a hefty promise to a world separated from Him because of sin. He knows we cannot fix things ourselves. We can't bridge the gap our transgressions have left. We can't even keep from wrongdoing for one day. But God, in His compassion and goodness, has made a way for us. He created hope for humanity. Our best efforts will never be good enough to overcome death and sin and bring restoration between the Creator and His creation. God knew the solution was on His shoulders and He came through, just like always. This promise can't be botched because it's about our eternal home.

The Lord's promises always come to fruition because His love is steadfast. He keeps His word because God isn't corruptible. We can have full confidence in this always.

Dear Lord, thank You for Your hefty promise of eternity in heaven for those who believe and obey because of their saving faith in Jesus. In His name, amen.

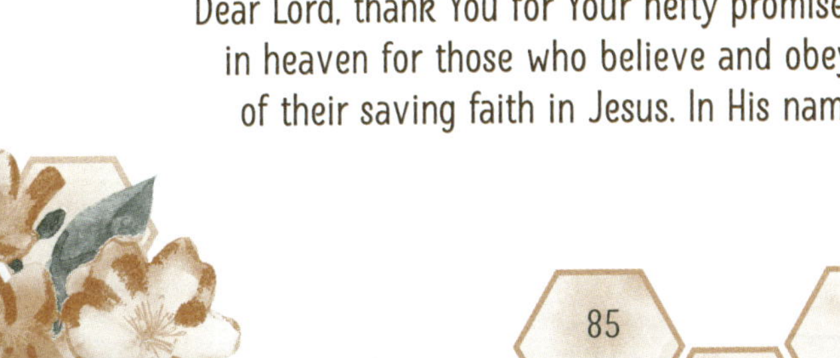

GROWING HOLINESS

But now that you have been emancipated from the death grip of sin and are God's slave, you have a different sort of life, a growing holiness. The outcome of that life is eternal life. The payoff for a life of sin is death, but God is offering us a free gift—eternal life through our Lord Jesus, the Anointed One, the Liberating King.

ROMANS 6:22–23 VOICE

What does a life of *growing holiness* look like? Believers are promised this once they accept Jesus as their Savior, releasing the death grip that sin has had on them. How do we live this promise?

So much of this is about our heart posture. It's knowing that God is sovereign and above all else. It's surrendering what we want for ourselves and embracing His perfect plans instead. It's trusting His timing and adopting a spirit of expectancy for His goodness to be revealed. It's committing to getting to know God better through reading the Word and looking for His hand in our lives. It's always being prayerful. And it's seeking His presence to guide us and our decisions.

Dear Lord, be with me as I pursue holiness, growing in my faith and glorifying Your name. Thank You for the promise of eternal life in heaven. In Jesus' name, amen.

THE PROMISE OF THE CROSS

We know this: whatever we used to be with our old sinful ways has been nailed to His cross. So our entire record of sin has been canceled, and we no longer have to bow down to sin's power.

ROMANS 6:6 VOICE

To believers, the power and promise of the cross means everything. It's where the Lord nailed our sinful ways, paying the price for our transgressions—past, present, and future. Jesus' death canceled the record of our sins. They're fully forgotten and there's no record of wrongs against us. We're no longer slaves to our sins and can walk in freedom. The cross made good on God's promise of redemption and brought with it the beginning of sanctification. It was a one-and-done act that began our transformation and secured our eternity in heaven.

Because of the cross, we can have a completely different earthly and eternal life. When we accept the free gift of salvation that it brings, our whole existence is drastically changed for the better. That is a divine promise made and kept by God. It's available to every person without discrimination. All we need to do is believe and confess that Jesus is Lord.

Dear Lord, thank You for the cross and its power in the life of a believer. In Jesus' name, amen.

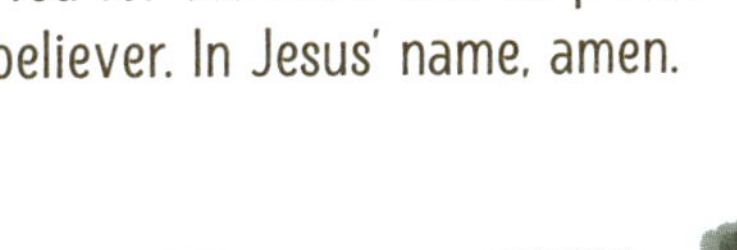

BLESSINGS FOR OBEDIENCE

That's the place where God set up rules and procedures; that's where he started testing them. God said, "If you listen, listen obediently to how God tells you to live in his presence, obeying his commandments and keeping all his laws, then I won't strike you with all the diseases that I inflicted on the Egyptians; I am God your healer."

Exodus 15:26 MSG

God was—and is—serious about wanting His followers to do as He commands, not in the spirit of a dictator but because of His all-encompassing love. He knows what is best for us and how we should live each day. God's commands aren't designed to squash us but to bring us freedom in meaningful and significant ways. They help us live a righteous life that glorifies God and is good for us. When we follow His commands, God promises to bless us.

Rules and procedures give us a much-needed blueprint to follow. We need godly guardrails to stay on the right road and not take a wrong turn that leads us away from God's will. Our pursuit won't be perfect, but being purposeful will delight His heart and lead to fulfilled promises.

Dear Lord, thank You for showing me how to follow Your will and ways. In Jesus' name, amen.

TANGIBLE LOVE

To rectify this situation, you must bring the entire tithe into the storage house in the temple so that there may be food for Me and for the Levites in My house. Feel free to test Me now in this. See whether or not I, the Eternal, Commander of heavenly armies, will open the windows of heaven to you and pour a blessing down upon you until all needs are satisfied.

MALACHI 3:10 VOICE

Today's verse is a rebuke to the Israelites for disobedience by not bringing their full tithes to the temple. They were then challenged to bring the whole tithe and watch as God blessed them with robust crops.

This verse is sometimes taken out of context to suggest that we are meant to continue the tithe today as believers. According to Matthew 5:17, the law was fulfilled in Jesus so we're no longer under the Mosaic Law. But that doesn't mean we shouldn't be generous with our time and treasure to support the church and Christian ministries locally and worldwide. God promises to bless us as we show tangible love and compassion to others.

Dear Lord, tender my heart to show tangible love to others. Help me share the resources You've given me to further Your kingdom work. In Jesus' name, amen.

TRUE TO HIS WORD

Blessed is the Eternal One who has given rest to His people Israel and who has fulfilled all His promises. He has been true to every last word of the promise He gave through His servant Moses.

1 Kings 8:56 voice

What a glowing endorsement of our God! It's a timely reminder that God keeps His promises. While the end results of some promises are yet to come, we can have confidence that they will be brought to fruition according to His will and timing. If God says He will do it, it will be done. If He says it will happen, it most certainly will. The Lord has a perfect history of fulfilling His Word. According to today's verse, He has been *true to every last word of the promise.* Let this encourage your heart right now.

What are you waiting for today? What are you trusting for with confident expectation? What promise has God made that you're believing for? Faithfulness is a cornerstone of every good relationship, and our relationship with the Lord is no different. We can trust that He will keep His promise.

Dear Lord, thank You for keeping promises to those who love and trust in You. Help me be confident in Your Word. In Jesus' name, amen.

PROMISE OF RESTORATION

"For I am the Lord—I do not change. That is why you are not already utterly destroyed, for my mercy endures forever. Though you have scorned my laws from earliest time, yet you may still return to me," says the Lord Almighty. "Come and I will forgive you."

MALACHI 3:6–7 TLB

As you read the Bible, you'll see how often the Israelites turned their backs on God and His commands. Yet He continually called them back into obedience, forgave them, restored them, and kept to the promise that they were His favored nation. Their spiritual rebellion never changed or challenged His love. It has and will continue to endure forever. Repeatedly, God extended grace rather than destroy the disobedient.

As His children, we also receive the promise of His kindness and generosity. God's compassion extends to us today—He cannot change. Even when we don't deserve it, the Lord is faithful and won't leave or forsake those who love Him. His grace will be extended as He pursues our return into His loving arms.

Dear Lord, knowing I can't work my way out of Your love and grace is a blessing. Thank You for second chances and for Your faithfulness to restore me. In Jesus' name, amen.

WE HAVE A PURPOSE

The Spirit of the Lord, the Eternal, is on me. The Lord has appointed me for a special purpose. He has anointed me to bring good news to the poor. He has sent me to repair broken hearts, and to declare to those who are held captive and bound in prison, "Be free from your imprisonment!"

ISAIAH 61:1 VOICE

We all have a calling on our lives, a special purpose designed just for us. We were created on purpose and for a purpose, and God will give us everything we need to fulfill that calling. He will anoint and appoint us, according to His will.

We may be called to mission work locally or across the globe. The Lord may ask us to write a book or stand on stage to share our testimony. He might ask us to give a sizeable donation for kingdom work. We may donate our time in a soup kitchen, visit nursing homes, participate in disaster cleanup, or help at a women's shelter. While it may feel scary and out of our comfort zone, God will be with us every step of the way.

If He calls you to it, the Lord promises to equip you for it.

Dear Lord, thank You for the promise of a purpose. In Jesus' name, amen.

PROMISES IN OUR GRIEF

As for those who grieve over Zion, God has sent me to give them a beautiful crown in exchange for ashes, to anoint them with gladness instead of sorrow, to wrap them in victory, joy, and praise instead of depression and sadness. People will call them magnificent, like great towering trees standing for what is right. They stand to the glory of the Eternal who planted them.

ISAIAH 61:3 VOICE

Today's verse promises restoration for those who mourn and grieve. Not only does God see you, but He will also meet you in those challenging moments. You may be sitting in the ashes of your broken relationships, financial ruin, health crisis, job loss, or bad choices, but the Lord has not abandoned you. Your sorrow won't last forever or pull you under. He will bring peace and gladness to your life again. He will give you joy and help you find reasons to praise, even in the midst of tragedy and failure. You can rest assured that He will see you through this. Others will be encouraged to see His faithfulness in your circumstances.

Jesus Christ sees the depth of grief and sadness and promises a crown in exchange. The Lord is ready to replace your ashes with beauty.

Dear Lord, meet me in my grief. In Jesus' name, amen.

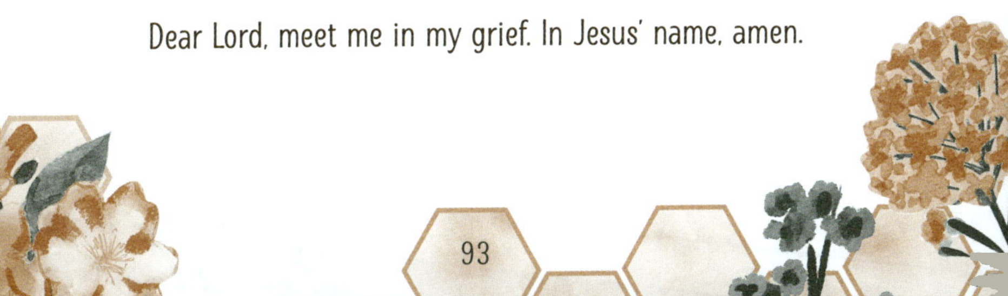

THE PROMISED REWARD FOR SUFFERING

For I, the Lord, love justice; I hate robbery and wrong. I will faithfully reward my people for their suffering and make an everlasting covenant with them. Their descendants shall be known and honored among the nations; all shall realize that they are a people God has blessed.

Isaiah 61:8–9 TLB

God's Word confirms an amazing promise to His people, including modern believers like us. The Lord clearly states that we will be rewarded for our suffering. The pain and grief we experience will not last forever. The rejection and betrayal won't take us out. This promise means that those difficult seasons aren't for naught. They will not prevail.

We know God uses these times to grow and mature our faith. We also know He sometimes uses them as a ripe training ground as we experience the natural consequences of bad choices. We learn patience and endurance. We learn grace. We learn about forgiveness. And we learn about God's goodness and how He brings hope and healing.

What a sweet gift to also know that these demanding times bring with them a blessing. That's something only the Lord can do.

Dear Lord, You always think of everything, and my heart is safe with You. I'm so glad I'm Yours forever. In Jesus' name, amen.

SMOOTHS AND STRAIGHTENS

Place your trust in the Eternal; rely on Him completely;
never depend upon your own ideas and inventions.
Give Him the credit for everything you accomplish, and He
will smooth out and straighten the road that lies ahead.
PROVERBS 3:5–6 VOICE

We desperately need God to help us in this lifetime. We need His guidance when we're confused, His prompting when we're feeling stuck in fear or worry, and His strength when we're at the end of our rope, out of ideas, and beaten down. We need His intervention because relying on ourselves can only get us so far. As believers, our trust must be secured in God so we can live with divine wisdom and discernment.

When we lean on Him rather than on our own understanding, a promise comes to fruition. Scripture says that reliance on God smooths and straightens the path ahead. In other words, we will see our next steps with clarity. He will reveal the way to go.

Let the Lord direct your decisions so they're wise and right. You may be smart, but His way is always the right way.

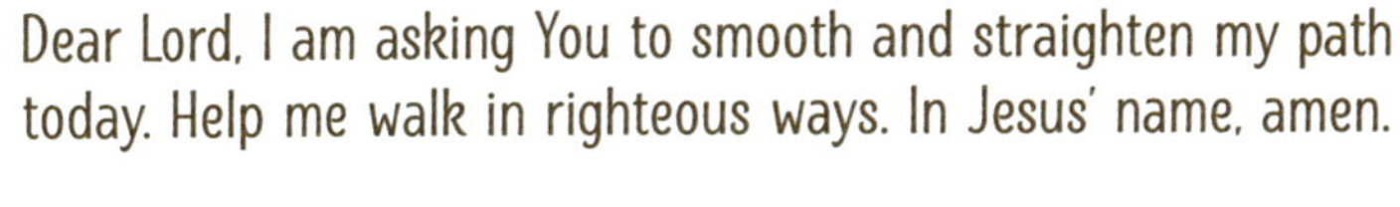

Dear Lord, I am asking You to smooth and straighten my path today. Help me walk in righteous ways. In Jesus' name, amen.

MERCY AND TRUTH

Stay focused; do not lose sight of mercy and truth; engrave them on a pendant, and hang it around your neck; meditate on them so they are written upon your heart. In this way, you will win the favor of God and others, and they will think well of you.

PROVERBS 3:3–4 VOICE

In Hebrew, the word *mercy* translates to loyal and faithful love, and the word *truth* means faithfulness. These words—mercy and truth (or love and faithfulness)—are often used in the Old Testament to signify making and keeping a promise.

Engraving them on a pendant and wearing them around your neck describes keeping them close and never being apart from them. These virtues should be part of a believer's life. Meditating allows them to sink deep into the core of who we are so they become our natural response to God and those around us.

These characteristics belong to Him; as believers, we can access them through our relationship. We can ask for them as we navigate this life. When we embrace mercy and truth, we will win His favor and the esteem of others. It's a promise we can count on.

Dear Lord, I want my life to bless others and glorify You through mercy and truth. In Jesus' name, amen.

WHAT'S RIGHT AND GOOD

And don't think you can decide on your own what is right and what is wrong. Respect the Eternal; turn and run from evil. If you depend on Him, your body and mind will be free from the strain of a sinful life, will experience healing and health, and will be strengthened at their core.

PROVERBS 3:7–8 VOICE

We get ourselves into big trouble when we depend on our own smarts. There are just too many factors that play into what we believe is good and bad, and we often get it wrong—sometimes innocently. That's why, as believers, we should ask God for wisdom. We need His divine discernment to keep us aligned with His will. Our crossroads between right and wrong should drive us to our knees as we pray and then patiently wait for direction.

Why? Because there's a promise attached to it. When we respect God and obey His commands, we'll experience freedom from the strain of sinful living, and we will find healing. It will strengthen us to stand strong in our faith.

Let's be women who seek God daily. Let's follow His lead and read the Word so we know what is right and good.

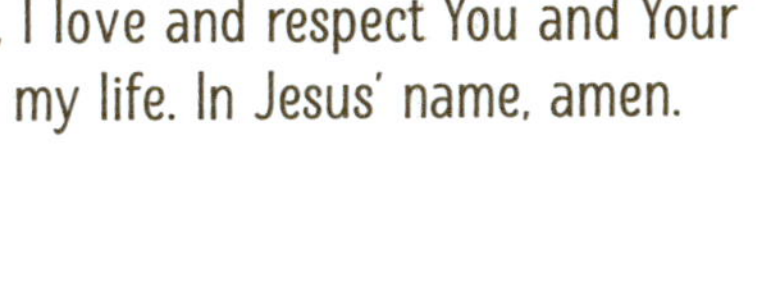

Dear Lord, I love and respect You and Your will for my life. In Jesus' name, amen.

WHY GOD CORRECTS YOU

My son, do not ignore the Eternal's instruction or lose heart when He steps in to correct you; because the Eternal proves His love by caring enough to discipline you, just as a father does his child, his pride and joy.

PROVERBS 3:11–12 VOICE

This is a tough truth to embrace because we don't like to be corrected, especially as adults. Being told we've stepped out of line hurts our pride and embarrasses us. When God corrects, however, it's an act of genuine love and proof that He cares for us as His daughters.

Remember, there's a difference between conviction and condemnation. The first is a sweet promise from the Lord, while the latter is a shaming tactic by the enemy. God's plan is to redirect you onto the right path, but the devil's plan is to derail you. One leads to goodness and the other to destruction. We want—and *need*—our Father to step in and correct us. We need His instruction to live a life that is pleasing to Him. Let's be grateful for His loving promise to guide our steps each day.

Dear Lord, it helps to know that You correct me because You love me so deeply. Help me embrace and appreciate it. In Jesus' name, amen.

WHEN CALAMITY STRIKES

Stay calm; there is no need to be afraid of a sudden disaster or to worry when calamity strikes the wicked, for the Eternal is always there to protect you. He will safeguard your each and every step.

PROVERBS 3:25–26 VOICE

Everyone who lives and breathes on planet earth faces calamity. Some more than others. Some seasons are tougher, while some feel more manageable. Certain tragedies can singlehandedly pull the rug out from under our feet and leave us breathless. But today's verses tell us to stay calm, and that's a tall order for even the most seasoned believer.

God promises that when the tough times come, He's there to protect you. You aren't alone, and you don't have to manage everything by yourself. You never will. These are the times we go to God and ask for help. We ask for wisdom and direction. We pour our hearts out and find comfort in His presence. This isn't a time to let fear run loose. Instead, you can stay calm, knowing you are safe and loved and the Lord is already at work.

Dear Lord, it's difficult to stay calm when I get knocked down. Mature my faith so I pray instead of panic. I'm a human with real emotions, but You're bigger than all of it. In Jesus' name, amen.

THE PROMISE OF GRACE

God treats the arrogant as they treat others, mocking the mockers, scorning the scornful, but He pours out His grace on the humble. In the end, the wise will receive honor, but fools will face humiliation.

PROVERBS 3:34–35 VOICE

All throughout the Bible, from Genesis to Revelation, we read about God's desire for a posture of humility from those who love Him. Proverbs 16:18 tells us "Pride precedes destruction; an arrogant spirit gives way to a nasty fall." In James 4:6, we're reminded that "God opposes the proud, but He pours out grace on the humble." Today's verse reveals His promise to pour out grace when we live with humility.

Be mindful of how you treat others. Take every opportunity to be kind and show respect. Don't ridicule or mock someone or treat them with disdain. It's possible to have hard conversations without disparaging people. You can advocate for yourself firmly and still speak the truth in love. When you choose to, be assured God sees it and will bless you. He'll keep His vow, just as He always does.

Dear Lord, help me avoid every inkling or desire to be hurtful to those around me. Even when I feel justified, help me to choose better. Let my words bring You glory. In Jesus' name, amen.

LET IT TAKE HOLD

Let the good news, the story you have heard from the beginning of your journey, live in and take hold of you. If that happens and you focus on the good news, then you will always remain in a relationship with the Son and the Father. This is what He promised us: eternal life.

1 JOHN 2:24–25 VOICE

The good news is that we can spend eternity in heaven because of Jesus' redemptive death on the cross. He stepped out of heaven and into the world to fulfill God's promise of eternal life to those who believe. Today's verses encourage us to let that beautiful truth take root in our lives.

How can we do that? We can make sure to stay focused on the good news of Jesus, meditating on it daily so it takes hold of us and transforms our lives according to His will. Let's spend time in the Word regularly, digging through scripture and learning more about God's goodness. Let's be prayerful about everything, inviting Him into our daily circumstances and keeping our attention on the eternal instead of the earthly. There's nothing of heavenly value for us here; thankfully, it's not our final home.

Dear Lord, let Your good news take hold of my heart. In Jesus' name, amen.

GOD'S CONSTANT FAITHFULNESS

"And yet My unfailing love of him will remain steadfast and strong. I will not be unfaithful to My promise. I will not violate My covenant, nor will I alter even one word of what My lips have spoken. These words I have pledged in My holiness once and for all, and I will not lie to David."

PSALM 89:33–35 VOICE

Today's scripture reading is part of a bigger contemplative song by Ethan the Ezrahite regarding God's choice of David as king and His covenant with him to establish an eternal dynasty. These few verses are a remembrance of what the Lord spoke through a vision to His faithful followers. It's His promise to love David and remain faithful to that pledge no matter what.

Let this message encourage you today. Our God is resolute in His word even now. Every promise mentioned in the Bible is unwavering. He's unchangeable. His pledges are unbreakable. His love for us is unshakable. No matter what we do wrong or how badly we mess up, God's faithfulness to believers is unflinching. Our Father will never walk away from those who love Him, and His Word is true forever.

Dear Lord, thank You for Your constant faithfulness to me and all believers, especially in a world that is uncertain and unreliable. In Jesus' name, amen.

SHARING GOD'S PROMISES

I will sing of Your unfailing love, Eternal One, forever. I will speak of Your faithfulness to all generations. I will tell how Your unfailing love will always stand strong; and how Your faithfulness is established in the heavens above.

Psalm 89:1–2 voice

The psalmist's heart is so full that he wants to share the promise of God's goodness with others. He wants to sing about the Lord's unfailing love, and the writer wants to talk about God's faithfulness. Have you ever been bursting at the seams about something like that?

If we truly understood who He is and what that means to believers, we'd be shouting about it from the rooftops. We'd want to tell everyone in the grocery aisles. Our social media would be flooded with powerful scripture and real-life testimonies. Our family and friends would be blessed by our unending enthusiasm and encouragement.

Don't shy away from sharing God's goodness with the world! You may be the person who plants the seed that will eventually bloom into a full-fledged faith. You may be the reason someone surrenders their will to His. As you unpack God's promises with others, your heartfelt words might lead them to eternal salvation.

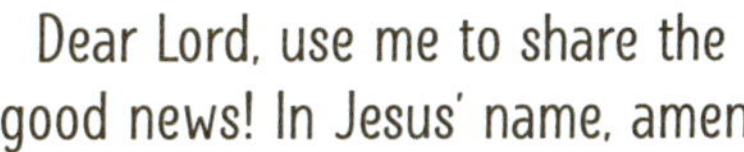

Dear Lord, use me to share the good news! In Jesus' name, amen.

FLAWLESS FAITHFULNESS

O Eternal God, Commander of heaven's armies, who is mighty like You? You are completely faithful; that's why we trust You. The ocean waters are at Your command. When violent waves rise up, You still them.

PSALM 89:8–9 VOICE

God's faithfulness is flawless. It doesn't waver or get watered down. It's not affected by feelings or emotions. It can't be revoked or tainted. It is forever consistent. That's a promise, and it's why we can trust God with anything and everything.

If you're struggling with finances, you can bet He knows it and will provide. If you are stirred up about work, you can expect Him to listen and guide your next steps. If you are stuck in a season of sinning and can't see a way out, you can anticipate God's help. When you're at a crossroads and confused about which path to take, you can believe that He'll bring clarity as you pray.

The Lord is Lord over everything, including the smallest details of your life. He is faithful to all, and that includes you as a believer. Cling to this promise and let it settle your anxious heart.

Dear Lord, thank You for being flawlessly faithful so I can wholeheartedly depend on You. In Jesus' name, amen.

A PROMISE THAT BLESSES

You are to honor your father and mother. If you do,
you and your children will live long and well in the land
the Eternal your God has promised to give you.
Exodus 20:12 voice

God's promise here must delight the hearts of parents around the world. It's a powerful vow we can point our children to in the right moments without shaming or browbeating them into submission. This isn't to be used as a weapon against a disobedient child but rather a verse meant to encourage. Let's make sure we use it responsibly.

Let's also remember that the road here may be a long one. Our children may have seasons of deep disrespect toward us. They may veer down a road that will most certainly lead to heartache. Our kids should have the space to make mistakes. They have the grace needed to navigate growing up in an imperfect world with imperfect parents. We can trust that God will use their journeys to help authenticate their faith and make it real and hardy.

When the time is right, and you want to affirm your kids and the way they honor you, point them to this promise. Share it to bless them.

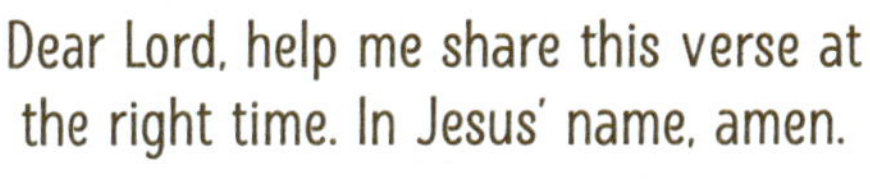
Dear Lord, help me share this verse at
the right time. In Jesus' name, amen.

A PROMISE FOR FUTURE GENERATIONS

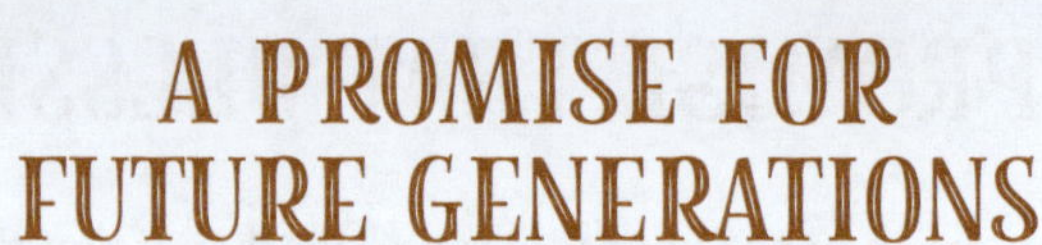

You are not to bow down and serve any image, for I, the Eternal your God, am a jealous God. As for those who are not loyal to Me, their children will endure the consequences of their sins for three or four generations. But for those who love Me and keep My directives, their children will experience My loyal love for a thousand generations.

Exodus 20:5–6 voice

Our lives of faith impact not only us but also our children and grandchildren. Based on how we choose to live here and now, they will either receive blessings or consequences. If we're faithful and focused on trying to live in a way that pleases the Lord, even in our imperfections, the next generation will reap God's goodness. However, if we're careless and worship what the world offers, our kids will feel the sting of our sinful ways.

This promise should help us fashion our days so that our words and actions serve the Lord. When you dig through scripture or set aside moments to pray earnestly, you bless both yourself and those to come. Your love and loyalty to God sow into their future.

Dear Lord, I'm learning that my life here matters and has ripple effects for the next generation. Help me to live with purpose. In Jesus' name, amen.

IT WON'T LAST FOREVER

After you have suffered for a little while, the God of grace who has called you [to His everlasting presence] through Jesus the Anointed will restore you, support you, strengthen you, and ground you. For all power belongs to God, now and forever. Amen.

1 PETER 5:10–11 VOICE

God promises that your suffering won't last forever. Even though it may seem like they won't ever end, the struggles you're facing are temporary. You may feel overwhelmed and think you can't deal with the pain or grief another day, but it will stop. The heartache may hit hard, but it's only for a little while. God is with you, even in the depths of your pain.

We're also promised that once the suffering has passed, God will heal our hearts through divine restoration. He will provide the support we need to find our firm footing once more. We will feel strong again, ready for whatever life brings forth. Instead of cowering in fear or waving the white flag in surrender, we'll stand tall in our faith. The Lord will empower us to live with the purpose He's called us to.

Dear Lord, help me endure suffering knowing
You are with me. In Jesus' name, amen.

THE CALL TO SURRENDER

So bow down under God's strong hand; then when the time comes, God will lift you up. Since God cares for you, let Him carry all your burdens and worries.

1 PETER 5:6–7 VOICE

This is a call to surrender, which isn't always an easy task. Why? Because we like to feel powerful, like we always know how to handle things perfectly on our own. Maybe we have lots of life experience and feel equipped to tackle life's challenges with hard-won wisdom. Maybe we're surrounded by a good and godly community of friends and family who will help us navigate the valleys. Or maybe we feel ashamed that we're here again and don't feel worthy to call out to God one more time. There's a sweet promise in store for those who choose to surrender anyway.

Today's verse tells us that when we bring our burdens to Him, bowing down in humility, the Lord will strengthen us. He will lift our heads and restore our vigor. While we often feel crushed under the weight of our worries, God never does. He promises to care for us as He straightens our crooked path. He will lighten our load and restore our peace and joy.

Dear Lord, I surrender all to You. In Jesus' name, amen.

VENTI-SIZED FAITH

In spite of all this, his faith in God's promise did not falter. In fact, his faith grew as he gave glory to God because he was supremely confident that God could deliver on His promise. This is why, you see, God saw his faith and counted him as righteous; this is how he became right with God.

ROMANS 4:20–22 VOICE

Abraham had a venti-sized faith, that's for sure. In Genesis 12:1, God said, "Abram, get up and go! Leave your country. Leave your relatives and your father's home, and travel to the land I will show you. Don't worry—I will guide you there." The Lord called him to leave the comfort of his home and all that was familiar and go. Abraham never hesitated. Maybe it was because in the next few verses, God promised that his obedience would lead to a successful journey, an abundance of blessings, and him being the father of many nations.

Abraham never doubted God would make good on His pledges, and it grew his faith. Even though he and Sarah were very old, making pregnancy impossible, he believed the Lord would do what He said He'd do, and God counted him as righteous. Talk about faith!

Dear Lord, give me faith like Abraham! In Jesus' name, amen.

THE PROMISE OF A NEW HEART

"I will plant a new heart and new spirit inside of you. I will take out your stubborn, stony heart and give you a willing, tender heart of flesh. And I will put My Spirit inside of you and inspire you to live by My statutes and follow My laws. Then you will live in the same land I gave your ancestors; you will be My people, and I will be your God."

Ezekiel 36:26–28 voice

In scripture, the heart is most often considered the thing that guides our choices and controls our will, feelings, and emotions. God's promise to plant a new heart inside us is what enables believers to better follow His commands. It helps us choose to behave in ways that glorify Him in our words and actions. It empowers us to align with what blesses the Lord so we can love, repent, forgive, and turn from evil.

When we accepted Jesus as our Savior, we went through an instantaneous and supernatural transplant. God made good on His promise to remove our stubborn heart of stone and replace it with a tender heart of flesh. He gave us the Holy Spirit to keep it that way while also growing our faith.

Dear Lord, thank You for my new heart! In Jesus' name, amen.

WE CAN'T COMPARE

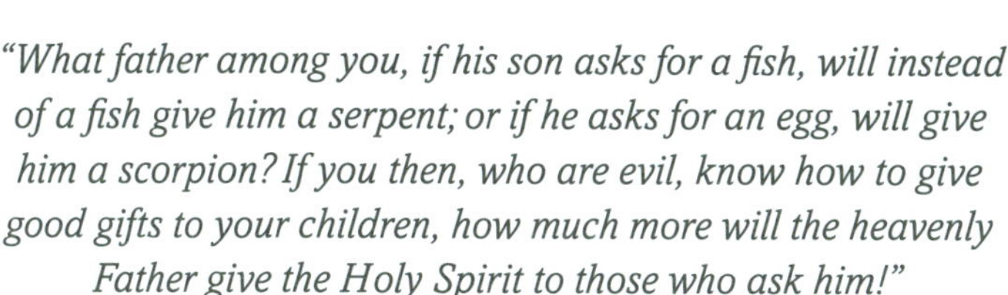

"What father among you, if his son asks for a fish, will instead of a fish give him a serpent; or if he asks for an egg, will give him a scorpion? If you then, who are evil, know how to give good gifts to your children, how much more will the heavenly Father give the Holy Spirit to those who ask him!"

LUKE 11:11–13 ESV

Today's verse points out that our best efforts can't come close to what God can offer. We try to love our friends with purpose, but sometimes we fall short. We put forth significant effort to care for our own kids, nieces, or nephews, but we can really mess things up. We commit to loving our husband or boyfriend, but our patience eventually runs out and we lose it. Even despite our grave imperfections, we try to give those we love good gifts.

God promises that He not only tries but succeeds—always. His efforts to show kindness and generosity never fail. His compassion is spot-on, with perfect timing. And His equipping, through the help of the Holy Spirit, will be flawless to those who ask.

Dear Lord, I appreciate that Your love never fails.
I can always trust that You will do exactly what You say.
This brings me great comfort. In Jesus' name, amen.

YOU ARE SEEN AND HEARD

So listen: Keep on asking, and you will receive. Keep on seeking, and you will find. Keep on knocking, and the door will be opened for you. All who keep asking will receive, all who keep seeking will find, and doors will open to those who keep knocking.

LUKE 11:9–10 VOICE

God promises that He always sees us. Our genuine efforts to find hope and help don't go unnoticed. Because we're deeply loved, God will bless us for pursuing Him with great intention. He doesn't hide from us. The Lord isn't too busy or unwilling to direct His attention our way. Instead, we're told to keep on asking with expectation, keep on seeking with a hopeful heart, and continue knocking regardless of barriers that may stand in our way. Because all who do will be blessed.

How does this promise offer you encouragement today? Where are you feeling unheard or weary in the continued asking? What answers have you been waiting for? What is the Spirit speaking into your heart about persistence in prayer?

Dear Lord, what a good reminder to stay vigilant in prayer and wait with expectation because You are faithful to respond at the right time and in the right ways. In Jesus' name, amen.

THE PROMISE OF TRANSFORMATION

All of Scripture is God-breathed; in its inspired voice, we hear useful teaching, rebuke, correction, instruction, and training for a life that is right so that God's people may be up to the task ahead and have all they need to accomplish every good work.

2 TIMOTHY 3:16–17 VOICE

Did you know there's a promise attached to God's Word? Hebrews 4:12 tells us it's "alive and moving; sharper than a double-edged sword; piercing the divide between soul and spirit, joints and marrow; able to judge the thoughts and will of the heart." Today's verse echoes that by reminding us that God uses scripture to train us for good and godly living. The promise is that He'll use the Bible to help transform us for the calling we've been created to walk out.

Knowing that, don't shortchange the time you spend digging through scripture. Don't rush through your reading just to cross it off the to-do list. Don't let distractions get in the way of your time in the Word. Let its truth sink into your heart so the Holy Spirit can mature your faith in new and necessary ways.

Dear Lord, I confess my lack of excitement about reading the Bible. Help me crave time in its pages where You promise to transform my life. In Jesus' name, amen.

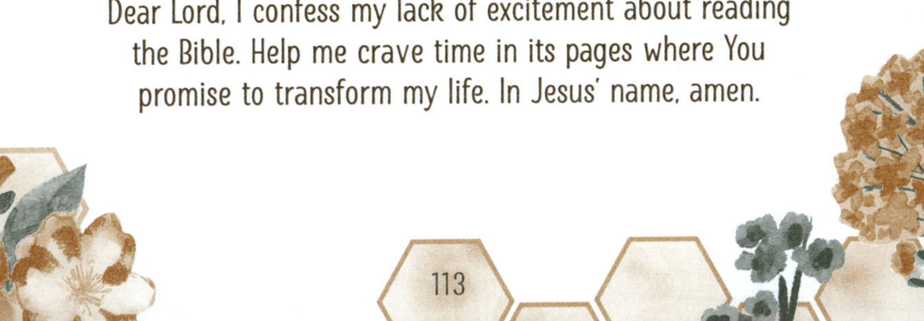

LIVING A GODLY LIFE

Although training your body has certain payoffs, godliness benefits all things—holding promise for life here and now and promise for the life that is coming. . . . This is what we work so hard for! This is why we are constantly struggling: because we have an assured hope fixed upon a living God who is the Savior of all humankind—especially all of us who believe.

1 TIMOTHY 4:8, 10 VOICE

We're promised that godliness benefits us both here and in eternity. How can we live a godly life? Titus 2:12 reveals that God wants us to turn away from carnal and sinful pleasures and live good, God-fearing lives. This means choosing to resist the world's enticement into wrongdoing and practicing self-control when faced with cultural influences. We take our thoughts captive and refuse to let our emotions control us. We control our tongue, taking Ephesians 4:29 to heart when it says "Don't let even one rotten word seep out of your mouths. Instead, offer only fresh words that build others up when they need it most."

Every bit of this requires God's strength and wisdom. We simply cannot do this on our own. Pray daily for His help.

Dear Lord, let me be a woman of faith whose life is marked by the pursuit of godliness. In Jesus' name, amen.

BORN AGAIN

Jesus replied, "With all the earnestness I possess I tell you this: Unless you are born again, you can never get into the Kingdom of God." "Born again!" exclaimed Nicodemus. "What do you mean? How can an old man go back into his mother's womb and be born again?" Jesus replied, "What I am telling you so earnestly is this: Unless one is born of water and the Spirit, he cannot enter the Kingdom of God."

JOHN 3:3–5 TLB

Many people have the wrong idea of how to come into a saving faith in Jesus. Whether through bad teaching or an innocent misunderstanding, countless people think they are saved, but they aren't. Even Nicodemus was confused and questioned Jesus, asking Him to further explain the process. We must be confident we've secured our eternity in heaven.

To be *born again* (to have a saving faith) means to believe in our hearts that Jesus is the Son of God who came to earth to redeem us, died on the cross to pay for our sins so they're no longer counted against us, and rose from the grave three days later. We must wholeheartedly believe and confess this and trust the Spirit to sanctify us daily. This is the *only* way.

Dear Lord, I believe! In Jesus' name, amen.

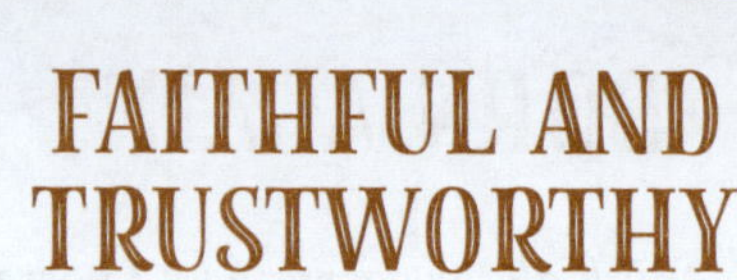

FAITHFUL AND TRUSTWORTHY

So now, may the God of peace make you His own completely and set you apart from the rest. May your spirit, soul, and body be preserved, kept intact and wholly free from any sort of blame at the coming of our Lord Jesus the Anointed. For the God who calls you is faithful, and He can be trusted to make it so.

1 THESSALONIANS 5:23–24 VOICE

No matter how we feel or what judgments we leverage against God, the Bible says He is faithful and trustworthy. Whatever negatives we may think of Him doesn't change the truth of who He is. Our opinions regarding God's divinity hold no weight.

His flawless Word reveals the Lord's nature and the unshakable promises He's made to humanity. We can confidently believe what it says without any doubt. It's timeless, so we can know the promises of His faithfulness and trustworthiness shared in its pages are for us here and now. God is who He says He is and will do what He says He will do.

How does this encourage your heart? In what current circumstances did you need this timely reminder? In a world of letdowns and upsets, you can always count on God to come through.

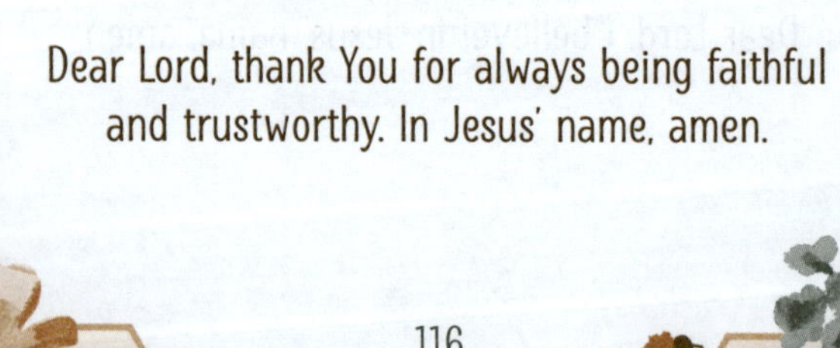

Dear Lord, thank You for always being faithful and trustworthy. In Jesus' name, amen.

PROMISED GIFT TO BELIEVERS

Reconsider your lives; change your direction. Participate in the ceremonial washing of baptism in the name of Jesus God's Anointed, the Liberating King. Then your sins will be forgiven, and the gift of the Holy Spirit will be yours. For the promise of the Spirit is for you, for your children, for all people—even those considered outsiders and outcasts—the Lord our God invites everyone to come to Him.

ACTS 2:38–39 VOICE

The Holy Spirit is a promised gift to believers. Often misunderstood, the Bible clearly states that God the Spirit is the third member of the Trinity. He is a divine person with a mind, will, and emotions.

John 14:26 says He will comfort, teach, and remind us of Jesus' words. According to Romans 8:26, He helps us with our daily problems and prays on our behalf when we can't find the words. 1 Corinthians 12:7–11 unpacks how the Spirit displays God's power through believers by giving us gifts designed to help the church. And Psalm 139:7–8 reveals His omnipresence in our lives and circumstances, no matter where we are. We are all invited to come to God in faith and receive the promised Holy Spirit.

Dear Lord, thank You for the Holy Spirit's unmatched work in my life. In Jesus' name, amen.

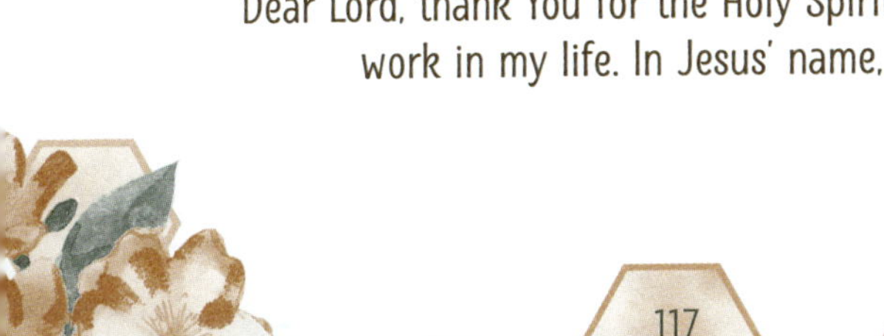

THE PROMISE OF TRUTH

We rest in this hope we've been given—the hope that we will live forever with our God—the hope that He proclaimed ages and ages ago (even before time began). And our God is no liar; He is not even capable of uttering lies.

TITUS 1:2 VOICE

God promises that His Word is truth. Proverbs 30:5 tells us that all His words are tried and true, and Psalm 12:6 says His promises are pure. Today's verse backs that up, reminding us He is not a liar. Let this be a breath of fresh air since we live in a world full of lies every day.

Because God is holy, He is perfect. He has the highest level of integrity and is, therefore, the only one who can set the standards for morals, ethics, and purity. When He speaks, God cannot lie, misrepresent, pervert, deceive, falsify, or distort. That means we can trust what He says and find hope in His promises. As believers, we should follow His example and be truthful in what we say. While we will never be able to walk this out perfectly, we can try with purpose to be honest in words and deeds.

Dear Lord, I am grateful that Your words are forever trustworthy. In Jesus' name, amen.

THE PROMISED FRUIT

The Holy Spirit produces a different kind of fruit: unconditional love, joy, peace, patience, kindheartedness, goodness, faithfulness, gentleness, and self-control. You won't find any law opposed to fruit like this.
GALATIANS 5:22–23 VOICE

Today's verses promise that the Holy Spirit will work in the lives of believers. He will grow our faith and produce the kind of fruit in us that matters most. Once we accept Jesus Christ as our Savior, the Spirit works in our lives meaningfully and significantly.

This process won't always be easy. There will be growing pains along the way. We may struggle and be challenged in situations we never imagined. It may hurt to change. That's okay! He is working to transform us into who we are created to be, and it will take time and grace. But we can trust the Holy Spirit to sanctify and purify according to God's perfect plan. He promises to produce love, joy, peace, patience, kindheartedness, goodness, faithfulness, gentleness, and self-control in our lives. Let it be. Let's surrender to the Spirit and let Him create these fruits in us.

Dear Lord, I want to be transformed into a woman of faith whose fruit is evident in my life. Let my heart embrace the Holy Spirit's work in me. In Jesus' name, amen.

THE PROMISE TO CARE

When I needed the Lord, I looked for Him; I called out to Him, and He heard me and responded. He came and rescued me from everything that made me so afraid.

PSALM 34:4 VOICE

Just as the psalmist experienced for himself, God is a good Father who promises to care for those who love Him. Whether we need comfort or strength, joy or peace, wisdom or discernment, courage or confidence, or for our hearts to be tendered toward others, the Lord will meet our needs in perfect and divine ways. We can trust He hears our prayers and will answer how He deems best.

What keeps you from calling out to God? Maybe you're embarrassed or struggling with pride. You might think your circumstances aren't important enough for Him to pay attention to, or that He is too busy to respond. Are you tired of asking? Does it feel like your prayers are bouncing off the ceiling? Maybe your pain is so strong that you're simply at a loss for words.

God heard and responded to the psalmist and will do the same for you. Be persistent in prayer and wait with expectation.

Dear Lord, I'm encouraged today and will trust in Your promise to care for me. In Jesus' name, amen.

GOD'S GOODNESS

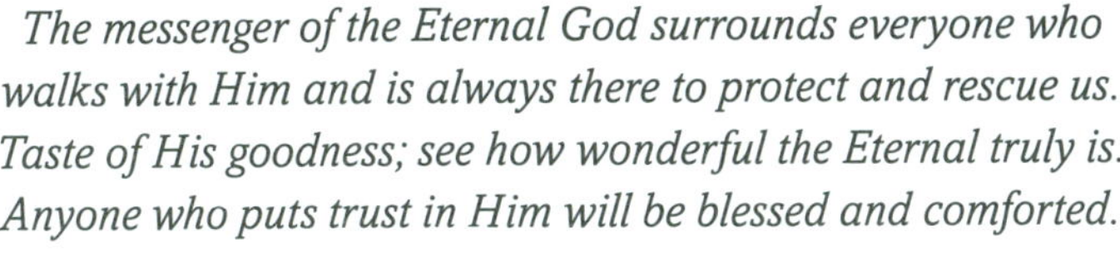

The messenger of the Eternal God surrounds everyone who walks with Him and is always there to protect and rescue us. Taste of His goodness; see how wonderful the Eternal truly is. Anyone who puts trust in Him will be blessed and comforted.

PSALM 34:7–8 VOICE

We are invited to taste and see God's goodness because it's always there, even in the hardest of times. When we feel defeated and overwhelmed, it's there. When we're grieving, it's there. When we're in chaos and confusion, His goodness is *still there*. Nothing can remove it. But it takes a steadfast faith to see it through those messy moments. It takes confidence and courage to grab on to God's goodness when we don't feel it. Try to remember times in the past when you felt His goodness on full display in your life. When we push through and trust Him, we're promised blessing and comfort.

Walking out your faith is a daily choice. There's no way around it. As believers, we can choose to look for His goodness regardless of our tough circumstances. It's there! Even when our situation looks hopeless, it will shine through.

Dear Lord, thank You for Your goodness! Help me look for it and trust in it. I know blessings and comfort will follow. In Jesus' name, amen.

PROMISES GO BOTH WAYS

Thorny branches and traps lie ahead for those who follow perverse paths; those who want to preserve themselves will steer clear of them. Teach a child how to follow the right way; even when he is old, he will stay on course.

PROVERBS 22:5–6 VOICE

Just as we will experience God's blessings for obeying His commands, we will also navigate undesirable consequences when we don't. In His great love, God lays these consequences out for us in His Word. He unpacks the positive promises that will come our way when we obey Him and the unfortunate promises that will happen when we instead follow our flesh. Every day, we make a series of decisions that will either set us up for blessings or blows.

As parents, aunts, godmothers, or trusted adults to kids, it's our privilege and burden to teach them what righteous living looks like, and what it does not. Let's be willing to point out thorny branches and traps in their pathways. Let's help them understand that their decisions matter. Let's demonstrate our love by taking every opportunity to teach about God's promises and what He expects.

Dear Lord, help me speak into the lives of kids around me, encouraging them to embrace Your promises. In Jesus' name, amen.

PROMISES FOR A WEARY SOUL

For the Eternal watches over the righteous, and His ears are attuned to their prayers. He is always listening. . . . When the upright need help and cry to the Eternal, He hears their cries and rescues them from all of their troubles. When someone is hurting or brokenhearted, the Eternal moves in close and revives him in his pain.

PSALM 34:15, 17–18 VOICE

In this hectic world, the promises unpacked in today's verses comfort our weary souls. They remind us that we are seen and celebrated by our God. We're not lost in the crowd. Instead, the Lord always watches over us. We are known by name. When we pray, He hears every word and sees every tear. We aren't ignored and left alone in our troubles. Our pain and heartache prompt God to move even closer to bring relief. A compassionate Father deeply loves us.

Don't let your struggles shut you down and keep you from praying. Don't look to the world to make you feel better or offer solutions. At the end of the day, God's promises are all we have and all we need.

Dear Lord, thank You for seeing and knowing me. No matter what the world brings my way, I trust You to bring me through to the other side. In Jesus' name, amen.

PROMISE TO RESCUE AND PROTECT

Hard times may well be the plight of the righteous—
they may often seem overwhelmed—but the Eternal rescues
the righteous from what oppresses them. He will protect
all of their bones; not even one bone will be broken.

Psalm 34:19–20 voice

What are you worried about today? What circumstances are stressing you out all day and keeping you awake at night? What upcoming decisions relentlessly hound you? What past bad behaviors continue to torment and tyrannize? What burdens feel too heavy to carry? What fears dominate your thoughts? Stop partnering with these oppressors. They aren't meant to be carried by you. Instead, God promises a rescue. He promises divine protection.

According to John 16:33, we will be plagued with trouble in this life. We will suffer because we try to live godly lives, and 2 Timothy 3:12 confirms this. 2 Corinthians 4:8–9 says believers will be cracked and chipped from afflictions on all sides. But God won't allow the world to win. Our circumstances may seem overwhelming, but we can confidently believe His promise to rescue and protect. Peace and comfort are available when we keep our eyes focused on the Lord.

Dear Lord, keep me close, especially when life's storms hit hard. You are my only hope. In Jesus' name, amen.

KEEP GOING

We are pressed on every side by troubles, but not crushed and broken. We are perplexed because we don't know why things happen as they do, but we don't give up and quit. We are hunted down, but God never abandons us. We get knocked down, but we get up again and keep going. These bodies of ours are constantly facing death just as Jesus did; so it is clear to all that it is only the living Christ within who keeps us safe.

2 CORINTHIANS 4:8–10 TLB

As believers, we have no choice but to get up and keep going when tough times come. We live with hope because of Jesus Christ. He will keep us safe and secure until we see Him face-to-face.

Too often, we live with a victim mentality and feel sorry for ourselves when things seem overwhelming. Rather than lean into God, we feel abandoned by Him. Why? The Bible clearly says that troubles will come. You will be pressed and perplexed. You'll get knocked down time and time again. But God promises you won't be crushed or broken. He will be with you every step of the way. You are safe with Him.

Dear Lord, I trust You to keep me safe and be with me in hard times. In Jesus' name, amen.

THE PROMISE OF PERFECTING

I am confident that the Creator, who has begun such a great work among you, will not stop in mid-design but will keep perfecting you until the day Jesus the Anointed, our Liberating King, returns to redeem the world.

PHILIPPIANS 1:6 VOICE

God promises to keep perfecting us until we reach heaven. While this is a huge blessing for believers, it can sometimes feel terrible in the moment. He will test us and bring trials into our lives to shape us into His image. The Lord will allow temptations to present themselves to authenticate our faith. We will be molded by circumstances and relationships. We'll be challenged to make the right choices, even when they're the hardest to make. He vows to finish the work set before Him. We may struggle, but we can trust God to have His hand in our lives daily until He returns or we go home to be with Him.

This is why we don't have to crumble under pressure or be stressed out when life gets hard. God hasn't turned His back on us. Instead, we can know without any doubt that He is at work and won't stop.

Dear Lord, thank You for the promise of perfecting me. Even though it often feels difficult and overwhelming, I trust You. In Jesus' name, amen.

EMBRACING

Don't run from tests and hardships, brothers and sisters. As difficult as they are, you will ultimately find joy in them; if you embrace them, your faith will blossom under pressure and teach you true patience as you endure. And true patience brought on by endurance will equip you to complete the long journey and cross the finish line—mature, complete, and wanting nothing.

JAMES 1:2–4 VOICE

We tend to run away from our problems. We'd rather ignore hard situations than face them. Finding solutions can feel daunting. We look for distractions instead, like books, movies, scrolling social media, or shopping. So often, we'd rather stick our heads in the sand than navigate those challenges. But scripture encourages us not to run but to embrace them instead.

Why is this God's plan? Because when we face them, our faith will grow. There's no other way to mature faith than through the pressure of trials. We'll learn patience and long-suffering, ultimately leading to joy and contentment. It's a supernatural process we can't explain, but it's a promise every believer can embrace because God is uncompromisingly trustworthy.

Dear Lord, help me embrace tests and hardships, trusting You to bless me through them. I know You only allow them for my good and Your glory. In Jesus' name, amen.

WE CAN'T DO IT

"I'd say it's easier to thread a camel through a needle's eye than get a rich person into God's kingdom." "Then who has any chance at all?" the others asked. "No chance at all," Jesus said, "if you think you can pull it off by yourself. Every chance in the world if you trust God to do it."

LUKE 18:25–27 MSG

When Jesus talked about a rich person having trouble getting into heaven, it had nothing to do with money itself. With the false sense of security that money offers, one may not see the need for a savior. The rich often become self-reliant, trying to buy their way out of messes they experience. But the truth is that even those without a copious amount of cash can miss the kingdom.

Jesus promised that we won't find our way into heaven on our own. We're not smart enough, clever enough, good enough, or strong enough. That's why we are humbled by the gift of Jesus and His work on the cross. He paid the price for the sin that would have kept us forever separated from God. Believing in Jesus and confessing it with our mouth secures a saving faith.

Dear Lord, thank You for Jesus and my salvation through Him. In Jesus' name, amen.

PROMISE OF DIVINE PROTECTION

You see, it's turning away from me that brings death to the simple, and it's self-satisfaction that destroys the fools. But those who listen to me now will live under divine protection; they can rest knowing they are out of harm's way.

PROVERBS 1:32–33 VOICE

Where are you desperate for divine protection today? Maybe you feel exposed because someone shared information that you asked to stay private. Maybe you're in the middle of divorce proceedings and worried about the settlement's fairness. Your bills might be piling up, and maybe you can't find a way to meet the financial demands. Or maybe you find yourself needing to advocate for a friend or family member and you're afraid of making mistakes or speaking out of turn. In times like these, be confident that God is trustworthy and keeps His promises. When you stay focused on Him, watching and listening for His leading, you can be assured the Lord will protect you and your efforts.

But when you instead lean into your own understanding and try to figure life out in your own strength, your best efforts will fall short. You will miss something, or you may feel outsmarted. Embrace God's divine protection. Let it bring you comfort.

Dear Lord, I trust You to help me in all things. In Jesus' name, amen.

LOVED AND FORGIVEN

Measure how high heaven is above the earth; God's wide, loving, kind heart is greater for those who revere Him. You see, God takes all our crimes—our seemingly inexhaustible sins—and removes them. As far as east is from the west, He removes them from us.

PSALM 103:11–12 VOICE

As believers, we are fully loved and completely forgiven. Our minds cannot begin to comprehend the depth, breadth, and width of God's compassion. We simply don't have the capacity as humankind to understand His goodness in our lives. Our human condition limits our minds. Although we cannot grasp it, the truth remains solid and unchanging. That means we can be confident in His promises to love us and remove our sins to the most significant degree possible. Our saving faith through Jesus Christ triggers this irreplaceable gift.

How would your life be different if you truly took today's verse to heart? Why is it difficult to believe you're so deeply loved? Do you have sins you think are unforgivable? Are you worried that God is mad at you? You can rest assured knowing you are fully loved and completely forgiven. It's an unbreakable promise.

Dear Lord, help me grasp that Your love is immeasurable and stable and that my sins are fully and forever forgiven. In Jesus' name, amen.

PROMISES FOR HERE AND NOW

He reaches deep into the pit to deliver you from death.
He crowns you with unfailing love and compassion like a king.
When your soul is famished and withering, He fills you with
good and beautiful things, satisfying you as long as you live.
He makes you strong like an eagle, restoring your youth.
PSALM 103:4–5 VOICE

There are so many powerful reasons for accepting Jesus as your personal Savior. Aside from the promise of eternity in heaven in God's presence, He has also made promises for the here and now that give us hope. Today's scripture outlines a few of them.

No matter how stressful our current situation is, the Lord will always lead us into wide, open spaces so we can breathe. He will respond when we ask for help. Nothing is too hard for Him. He will always show us the path forward. When we're overwhelmed by our circumstances and worried about how it will all work out, He'll bring necessary restoration through His goodness. God will strengthen us and settle our spirits, restoring contentment in our hearts supernaturally and abundantly. We can count on Him for restoration, especially when we need it most.

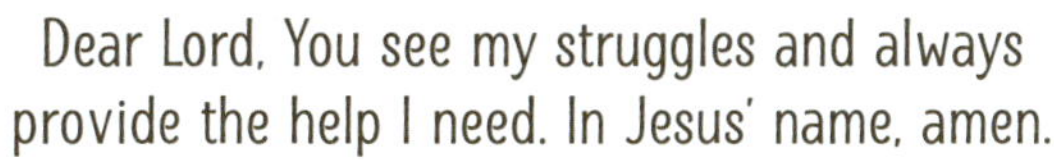

Dear Lord, You see my struggles and always provide the help I need. In Jesus' name, amen.

SECURE IN GOD'S LOVE

The Eternal is compassionate and merciful. When we cross all the lines, He is patient with us. When we struggle against Him, He lovingly stays with us—changing, convicting, prodding; He will not constantly criticize, nor will He hold a grudge forever.

PSALM 103:8–9 VOICE

This is a remarkable passage of scripture! Have you truly considered how amazing God is and the depth of His compassion? His promise to love us is unwavering. He's merciful even when we blast through every godly guardrail. He remains patient when we fight against His will. God lovingly keeps us close, even as we rebel against the Spirit's correction. No matter what we do, what we feel, or what we plot, the Lord is consistent with us in every way. He won't verbally berate us or hold our shortcomings against us. We are secure in His love.

We can anchor ourselves to this promise. While we pursue righteous living, our human condition often gets in the way. But this truth can tender our hearts and give us confidence in God's goodness. It will strengthen our faith and settle our anxiousness if we embrace it. How does this promise bring you hope?

Dear Lord, thank You for promising to never give up on me! In Jesus' name, amen.

NOT A SINGLE ONE

So He gave them rest from war on every side as He had sworn to their ancestors; none of their enemies still stood against them, for the Eternal had delivered them all into their hands. Not a single one of all the good promises that He had made to the house of Israel went unfulfilled; all of them came to pass.

JOSHUA 21:44–45 VOICE

If you ever struggle to believe God will keep His promises, just look at the nation of Israel. They messed up royally, made a multitude of bad decisions, turned their backs on Him, and worshipped false gods, yet He held true to every promise. Time and time again, He did exactly what He said He would do. He never wavered in His love for the Israelites. Without fail, the Lord kept His word despite their continued disobedience. Every promise made for His children remains intact and will come to pass at the right time.

Be encouraged! You can be confident that no pledge of God's will go unfulfilled. If written in His Word, it's a timeless vow you can trust, even though it was made thousands of years ago. The Lord doesn't change, and neither do His promises.

Dear Lord, I'm richly blessed that Your promises are steadfast. In Jesus' name, amen.

THE GIFT OF COMMUNITY

In the same way that iron sharpens iron, a person sharpens the character of his friend.

PROVERBS 27:17 VOICE

God created us for community. We're made to be surrounded by like-minded people who love the Lord. It's an important part of a believer's life. Community is how we share encouragement with one another and how we stand strong in tough times. These are the friends and family we link arms with when we are knocked down by unwelcome news. They remind us of God's goodness when we need to refocus our hearts. Community allows us to love and serve others meaningfully as His hands and feet. Together, we share godly wisdom, belly laughs, and comforting moments. Today's verse says that even our character will be sharpened by our community.

This is a blessing and a promise that should delight our hearts because God thought of everything. He made a way for us to be deeply cared for here and in heaven. We're not left alone to figure things out and trudge through life without support. Instead, we have people to walk with and help us live righteously. Who makes up your community?

Dear Lord, thank You for people who love and support me. Help me be a good and godly community member in return. In Jesus' name, amen.

HE WILL PROTECT

Like a bird protecting its young, God will cover you with His feathers, will protect you under His great wings; His faithfulness will form a shield around you, a rock-solid wall to protect you.

PSALM 91:4 VOICE

It's good to know that God has our backs in a dark world that often feels dangerous. He protects against evil and will keep us sheltered and shielded on all sides when the storms of life hit. There's nothing stronger or more durable than the Lord's vow to safeguard those who love Him. We can always count on that promise.

Here's where that gets tricky. This promise of protection doesn't mean we won't have trouble. We will face disease and financial struggles. We will lose jobs and loved ones. We will have to navigate the sting of rejection and betrayal. There will be times when we're hurt emotionally and physically. Sometimes life will feel too heavy to bear. But God knows our limits.

We live in a fallen world where difficulties abound, but He will protect you even when you're experiencing extreme hardship. You can trust that!

Dear Lord, thank You for knowing my limits and protecting me from suffering past that point. You always have my best interest in mind. In Jesus' name, amen.

TRUSTING GOD'S PROMISES

He who takes refuge in the shelter of the Most High will be safe in the shadow of the Almighty. He will say to the Eternal, "My shelter, my mighty fortress, my God, I place all my trust in You." For He will rescue you from the snares set by your enemies who entrap you and from deadly plagues.

PSALM 91:1–3 VOICE

When we choose to rely on God as our source for all things, we will find safety there. Trusting in someone we cannot see may be a scary proposition. It may be challenging to assume the Lord will show up, even though He has every other time. Or maybe we know He will meet our needs, but we're worried it won't be in the way we want or the timing we hope for. Our doubt doesn't change His divinity.

There is always a blessing that comes from obedience. This is mentioned countless times in the Bible. Out of His deep delight, God rewards a believer who places their trust in Him. He understands how difficult it can be to do so. He knows every fear and worry giving up control brings. But God always keeps the promises He makes.

Dear Lord, help me trust You and Your promises. In Jesus' name, amen.

HE WILL MEET OUR NEEDS

"Because he clings to Me in love, I will rescue him from harm; I will set him above danger. Because he has known Me by name, he will call on Me, and I will answer. I'll be with him through hard times; I'll rescue him and grant him honor."

PSALM 91:14–15 VOICE

Having an intimate relationship with God reaps so much goodness. It's mind-blowing because we never expected the profound and immeasurable ways He would bless us. Our saving faith has opened doors we didn't even know were there. The heavenly Father promises to meet our needs according to His perfect plans.

God is moved to action when we need rescue from the enemy's tangles or safety in the face of danger. He will offer guidance when we're confused and looking for answers regarding relationships, finances, careers, health, or the next step in our circumstances. When caught in the storms of life, being tossed back and forth, we are promised His presence. There is no situation or struggle where God won't go with us. His love for us won't ever be compromised.

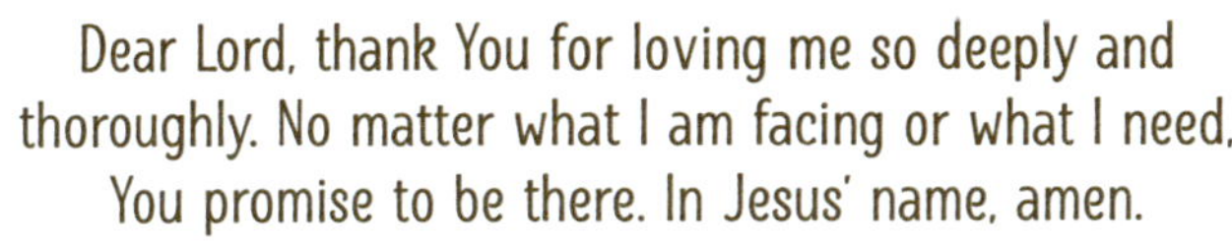

Dear Lord, thank You for loving me so deeply and thoroughly. No matter what I am facing or what I need, You promise to be there. In Jesus' name, amen.

A CONFIDENCE BUILDER

Whenever I walk into trouble, You are there to bring me out. You hold out Your hand to protect me against the wrath of my enemies, and hold me safely in Your right hand. The Eternal will finish what He started in me. Your faithful love, O Eternal One, lasts forever; do not give up on what Your hands have made.

PSALM 138:7–8 VOICE

The promises in these verses are a confidence builder. They enable us to trust God with our lives because we know He is at work. For believers, this keeps us from the proverbial performance treadmill, trying to fix ourselves. It reminds us that God is our protector and will deliver us from evil. It affirms His steadfast love for His creation. It allows us to rest knowing He is faithful to complete a good work in us.

Let this bring much-needed comfort to your heart today. Let it anchor you in all the right ways. In this crazy world that feels unstable, unsafe, and unfair, it's good for us to remember that our God is unshakable. He's trustworthy. The Lord will do what He says He will do. Because of that, we can experience security because He's always with us.

Dear Lord, You are my everything. In Jesus' name, amen.

UNFAILING LOVE

I bow before You, looking to Your holy temple, and praise Your name, for Your unfailing love and Your truth; for You have placed Your name and Your word over all things and all times. On the day I needed You, I called, and You responded and infused my soul with strength.

PSALM 138:2–3 VOICE

God's unfailing love is a promise to all believers. It's dependable. It's reliable. It's constant. Because of that, He will meet us in our darkest hours and shine His light. He will guide us through the valleys. He'll direct our steps when the road is rocky. God's presence will be with us always.

When our relationships are falling apart, our finances are at rock bottom, our health is at a critical point, or our hearts are broken by betrayal, God will help. Our cry for intervention will reach His holy ears, and the Lord will respond. He promises to infuse our soul with strength, providing whatever is necessary at that moment. We may not even know what that true need is, but God does.

Before you reach for any worldly remedy, pray. Before you unpack your fear and worry with a friend, pray. The Father's love for you is unfailing.

Dear Lord, I will trust in Your unfailing love. In Jesus' name, amen.

FULFILLED PROMISE

"When the Holy Spirit, who is truth, comes, he shall guide you into all truth, for he will not be presenting his own ideas, but will be passing on to you what he has heard. He will tell you about the future. He shall praise me and bring me great honor by showing you my glory."

JOHN 16:13–14 TLB

The Holy Spirit is a fulfilled promise for every believer. Once we accept Jesus as our personal Savior, the Spirit takes up residency. He's a constant companion, helping us make good and godly choices. Yes, He has a great purpose!

The Bible says He is the truth, and the Spirit will guide us into it each day. His knowledge comes from God, who knows and sees all we're walking through. He'll enable us to discern right from wrong. The Spirit isn't working alone, but is instead relaying the Lord's heart to us. His job is to mature our faith and reveal God's glory in our lives.

Are you listening for His leading? Are you seeking His direction in your circumstances? Do you seek truth in the Word and through prayer?

Dear Lord, Your Holy Spirit is a fulfilled promise that blesses me every single day. Thank You. In Jesus' name, amen.

THE PROMISE TO OVERCOME

"But the time is coming—in fact, it is here—when you will be scattered, each one returning to his own home, leaving me alone. Yet I will not be alone, for the Father is with me. I have told you all this so that you will have peace of heart and mind. Here on earth you will have many trials and sorrows; but cheer up, for I have overcome the world."
JOHN 16:32–33 TLB

Jesus knew tough days were coming for His disciples. He also knew that their only chance at having peace through these difficulties was a strong relationship with Jesus. Trying to handle the hardships on their own would be impossible, and He knew the intense persecution headed their way. The same is true for us today.

Jesus conquered the world. What does that mean for believers? According to John 14:27, we can experience peace over anxiety and fear. We have victory over sin, according to Ephesians 2:4–6. 1 John 4:4 tells us we can face persecution because we have the Holy Spirit in us, who is stronger than anything the world throws our way. And we're fitted for every earthly battle with heavenly armor, according to Ephesians 6:10–17.

Dear Lord, You defeated the enemy's plans at every turn and equipped us to be victorious through You. What a blessing! In Jesus' name, amen.

THE PROMISED MEDIATOR

This is why Jesus is the mediator of the new covenant: through His death, He delivered us from the sins that we had built up under the first covenant, and His death has made it possible for all who are called to receive God's promised inheritance.

HEBREWS 9:15 VOICE

A mediator is someone who works with opposing sides to reach a settlement. They help dissolve disputes and find resolutions. Jesus Christ was tasked with that role between the Creator and His creation. He was the only one who could make a way.

In our case, this dividing issue was sin. It's rebellion against God and His holiness, and our transgressions are punishable by separation from Him and eternal death in hell. Our Father couldn't stand this divide and sent Jesus to bridge the gap sin left. God promised that His Son's death on the cross would satisfy His wrath and be the only acceptable atonement for our wrongdoing, once and for all.

Thanks to our mediator, we can be together forever with the Lord. Our sins—past, present, and future—are forgiven and removed. We've been delivered from them.

Dear Lord, thank You for the gift of Jesus as mediator and Savior. I recognize that I'd be forever lost without Him. In Jesus' name, amen.

CHOSEN AND TREASURED

"You are eyewitnesses of all that I did to the Egyptians. You saw how I snatched you from the bonds of slavery and carried you on eagles' wings and brought you to Myself. Now if you will hear My voice, obey what I say, and keep My covenant, then you—out of all the nations of the world—will be My treasured people. After all, the earth belongs to Me."

EXODUS 19:4–5 VOICE

God is speaking to Moses on Mount Sinai, telling him what to say to the Israelites waiting at the mountain's base. He's calling them to follow His commands and keep His covenant. God is reminding them of His faithfulness, how He freed them from bondage, and how He cared for them in the wilderness. The Lord wants them to recognize their covenant relationship to date and know it will continue. They are His chosen, treasured people.

As believers today, we are also chosen and treasured by our Father. We too have a covenant with God because we believe in Jesus as His Son, who died and rose three days later, paying the price for our sins on the cross. That promise of salvation is forever.

Dear Lord, what a privilege to be chosen and treasured. You're faithful to Your promises, and I trust You. In Jesus' name, amen.

THE PROMISE OF HIS LOVE

And I pray that Christ will be more and more at home in your hearts, living within you as you trust in him. May your roots go down deep into the soil of God's marvelous love; and may you be able to feel and understand, as all God's children should, how long, how wide, how deep, and how high his love really is; and to experience this love for yourselves, though it is so great that you will never see the end of it or fully know or understand it. And so at last you will be filled up with God himself.

EPHESIANS 3:17–19 TLB

God's love is so expansive that we will never be able to find its borders. We can't see its beginning, and we'll never see its end. Scripture even states that the love of Christ is beyond our knowledge, and only with His power will we be able to grasp its reality. Let this encourage you today!

That means we will never exhaust God to the point of Him giving up on us. We won't ever push Him too far. Our messy moments can't scare Him off, and our propensity towards drama isn't a deterrent. God won't forget us or push us down His divine to-do list. We are fully loved right now, and nothing will ever change that. It's a promise from God Himself.

Dear Lord, keep close to me as I walk through this life. I find comfort in Your unwavering love. In Jesus' name, amen.

PEACE PROMISED

Those who love Your law have an abundance of peace,
and nothing along their paths can cause them to stumble.
Psalm 119:165 voice

Believers are promised abundant peace because of our commitment to and love for God's Word. The more time we invest in studying it, the deeper our affinity for the Bible will become. We will be touched by real-life accounts of people whose lives intersected with Jesus. We'll be mesmerized by the major and minor prophets and how their divinatory words came to be. Our hearts will be challenged and comforted by certain scriptures and reading them at the right time can encourage us in our circumstances. We will find godly guardrails of wisdom to help us live a righteous life, pleasing to God. We can find comfort in knowing His expectations, and He will provide the strength we need to make them our reality. As we count on the Bible as our blueprint for holy living and our roadmap for a relationship with God, a supernatural peace will follow.

Are you in God's Word daily? Are you committed to regularly reading its pages and soaking in its goodness? If you want peace, you will find it there.

Dear Lord, I want the promise of peace that comes
from loving Your Word. In Jesus' name, amen.

THE PROMISE OF HAPPINESS

Happy are the people who walk with integrity, who live according to the teachings of the Eternal. Happy are the people who keep His decrees, who pursue Him wholeheartedly. These are people who do nothing wrong; they do what it takes to follow His ways.

PSALM 119:1–3 VOICE

If you're a believer struggling with joy and happiness, why not take inventory of your faith journey based on today's verse? According to Romans 8:1, there's no condemnation for those in Christ Jesus. Think about it. Are you walking with integrity in your personal and work life? Are you being honest and thoughtful in your actions? Are you purposeful to follow God's commands, albeit imperfectly? Do you pursue God passionately and enthusiastically, inviting Him into your day? If you're falling short, that may be the reason your mood is struggling.

God promises joy and happiness when we live honestly and humbly, obey His commands, and seek a relationship with Him. Perfection isn't the goal; it's living with purpose and passion for Him and His commands.

Talk to the Lord and repent if necessary. Ask for His help to live righteously. Let divine joy and happiness surround you.

Dear Lord, I confess my failings to live as You decree. Help me live in such ways that bring holy happiness. In Jesus' name, amen.

PROMISED GRACE

For it's by God's grace that you have been saved. You receive it through faith. It was not our plan or our effort. It is God's gift, pure and simple. You didn't earn it, not one of us did, so don't go around bragging that you must have done something amazing.

EPHESIANS 2:8–9 VOICE

Our salvation comes through faith alone. We can't earn it by how hard we work. Our good actions won't secure it. How we treat others has no bearing on it. Our thought life can never be pure enough. We can't follow a man-made formula to warrant it. In our sinful nature, we won't ever be able to produce righteousness ourselves. Frankly, we don't deserve it. Left to our own devices, we're in trouble.

God promises that it's His grace that saves us. When we believe that Jesus is His only Son, who stepped off the throne and into the world, died on the cross to save us from our sins, and rose three days later, we have a saving faith. Christ came down to redeem us and make a way back to the Father. We are called to believe and confess this. When we do, our eternity in heaven is guaranteed.

Dear Lord, I believe and confess that You are Lord! In Jesus' name, amen.

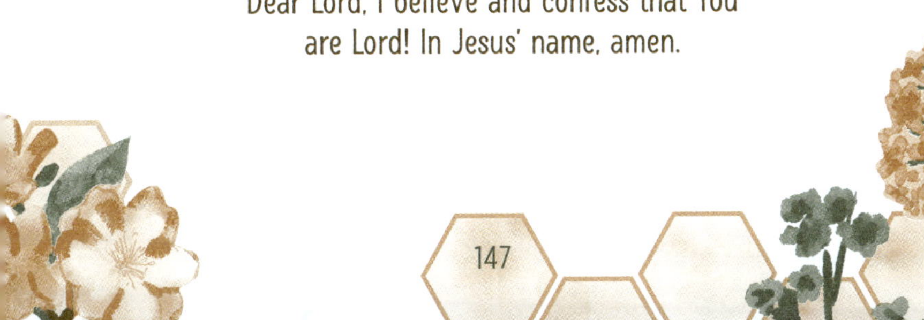

OBEYING THE IFS

"But if you genuinely change your ways and stop what you are doing; if you deal with each other fairly; if you don't oppress foreigners, orphans, and widows; if you don't shed the blood of the innocent in this land; and if you don't practice the self-destructive worship of other gods; then I will let you live forever in this land I promised your ancestors long ago."

JEREMIAH 7:5–7 VOICE

That's a lot of *ifs*. The Israelites are being told what God expects from them. He's revealing the blueprint of obedience that comes with a promise, and it sets them up for a beautiful future and land to call home forever. But they had to change their ways. They had to treat one another kindly. They needed to stay true to the Lord. While God knew they were flawed, He was looking for intentionality.

What is the Lord asking of you? What behaviors and attitudes is He hoping to see? What needs to change in you before He brings abundant blessings? What *ifs* has God laid out? His love and compassion for you are never conditional, but His blessings are.

Dear Lord, help me listen to and obey Your leading so I please You and set myself up to reap the rewards of Your goodness. In Jesus' name, amen.

COUNTED AS RIGHTEOUS

The promise given to Abraham and his children, that one day they would inherit the world, did not come because he followed the rules of the law. It came as a result of his right standing before God, a standing he obtained through faith.

ROMANS 4:13 VOICE

What matters the most is being in a right relationship with God. That's where our security comes from. While we may feel satisfied when the house is clean, the laundry is done, our bank balance is robust, there's gas in the car, and the pantry is stocked with food, this doesn't get us closer to God. Being organized and following the rules are good, but the Lord is looking for something different from His followers.

God counted Abraham righteous because he trusted and followed Him. That's it. Rather than being worried about the things of the world or his own personal comfort, Abraham spent time with God and obeyed, even with little information on the path forward.

Let's be women who are counted as righteous and see God's promises come to pass. Let's please Him through obedient faith. He is good and His plans are perfect.

Dear Lord, I trust You to lead my life. Help me obey You and be counted as righteous. In Jesus' name, amen.

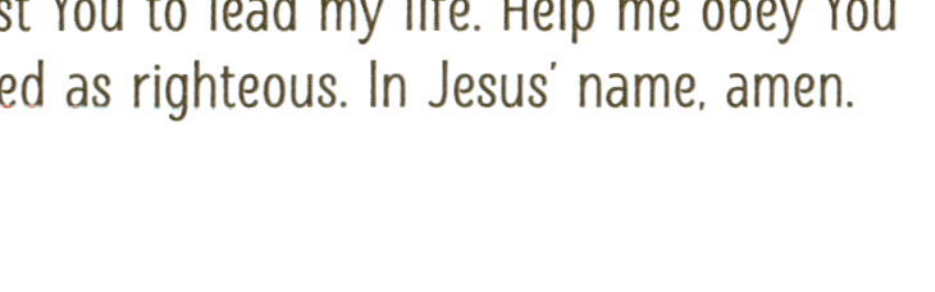

THE WICKED WORLD

Pray also that we would all be rescued from the snares of harmful, wicked people—after all, not all people are believing. Still, the Lord is true to His promises; He will hold you up and guard you against the evil one.

2 THESSALONIANS 3:2–3 VOICE

There is so much evil running rampant in the world today. It's the enemy's playground, and he does everything possible to discourage and disappoint believers. We encounter angry and wicked people on the highway, at the grocery store, in the neighborhood, at the office, and even in church. It's not hard to see that tensions are running high. So often, we just want it to stop.

John 16:33 reminds us that in this world, we will have trouble. We're not promised an easy, problem-free life. Before our feet hit the floor in the morning, we should pray for God's protection. Let's pray for discernment so that if it's possible to avoid trouble, we will. Let's also remember to ask for help when we find ourselves trapped in the enemy's snares. God promises to hold us up because He loves us. He promises to guard us because He's a good, good Father.

Dear Lord, thank You for promising to help me when I'm overwhelmed by the wicked world. In Jesus' name, amen.

ENDLESS COMPASSION

Yet there is one ray of hope: his compassion never ends. It is only the Lord's mercies that have kept us from complete destruction. Great is his faithfulness; his loving-kindness begins afresh each day. My soul claims the Lord as my inheritance; therefore I will hope in him.

LAMENTATIONS 3:21–24 TLB

It would blow our minds to see how many times God has protected us from troubles without us even knowing it. There have been close calls we never recognized. We've narrowly escaped the enemy's grasp and come within inches of devastation, but God intervened without our knowledge. He does this because He loves us so deeply.

Today's verses reveal a promise that the well of His compassion is endless. His mercy can't be drained, and His faithfulness is a forever pledge to believers. God's kindness is refreshed every day, so it's always available when we need it. Our eternity is secured in heaven because of Jesus, so we can live with that hope here and now. He will take care of us on earth and in our eternal home.

Dear Lord, I know Your promise of compassion has blessed me more times than I know. You take care of me here, and I will be in Your sweet presence in heaven one day. Thank You. In Jesus' name, amen.

HE REMAINS FAITHFUL

Even when we are too weak to have any faith left, he remains faithful to us and will help us, for he cannot disown us who are part of himself, and he will always carry out his promises to us.

2 TIMOTHY 2:13 TLB

Even when we mess up and lack faith in our circumstances, Paul reminds us that God will always remain faithful. He will continue to help us instead of turning away in frustration. The Lord will never disown us, because we are now part of Him through our faith in Jesus. Once we receive that saving faith, God promises to be with us always. Romans 8:38–39 reminds us that we can't be separated from His love. He will keep His word.

Don't let a lack of faith lead you to believe God is waiting to toss you aside when you make mistakes. He's not looking for reasons to revoke your salvation. Your bad choices, mean-spirited responses, grudges, hurtful words, inappropriate thoughts, and bad attitude won't make God second-guess His love. You are His. Repent and return to the Lord, fully embracing His promise to remain faithful to you always.

Dear Lord, it's a blessing to know You will always remain faithful, just as promised. In Jesus' name, amen.

THE SEAL OF GOD

Regardless of what they do or say, God's foundation is strong and firmly in place, etched with this seal: "The Lord knows the ones who belong to Him," and, "Everyone who invokes the name of the Lord ought to stop doing what they know to be wrong."

2 TIMOTHY 2:19 VOICE

Earlier in this chapter, Paul encourages Timothy to stay away from the ungodly because they only lead to a godless lifestyle. Their false doctrines may even cause one to turn their back on God, just as they are trying to do. Those whose faith isn't well grounded are especially vulnerable.

But God knows those who are His, and He promises to keep them close. Paul mentions the seal because when you accept Jesus as your Savior, you are marked in Him by that seal, which is the Holy Spirit. The Spirit is a deposit on our promised inheritance.

Be comforted in knowing that you are saved, sealed, and secure as God's child. It's a guarantee that can't be taken away, even when you make mistakes. You're His forever, both here on earth and in eternity.

Dear Lord, I am humbled by this promise. It settles my anxious heart to understand that I am forever saved, sealed, and secure as Your child. In Jesus' name, amen.

ALWAYS TRUSTWORTHY

And he guarantees right up to the end that you will be counted free from all sin and guilt on that day when he returns. God will surely do this for you, for he always does just what he says, and he is the one who invited you into this wonderful friendship with his Son, even Christ our Lord.

1 CORINTHIANS 1:8–9 TLB

God always does what He says. When we struggle, it can be hard to believe, rely on, and trust that to be true.

Hebrews 13:5 says the Lord will never leave or forsake us, but maybe we've felt like He has before. John 3:16 reminds us how deeply we are loved, but sometimes we don't feel it. John 15:14 says we are friends with Jesus if we keep His commands, but we may feel far from Him even when we do. It may seem as if God's Word has failed, but it doesn't change the fact that He is trustworthy.

Matthew 24:35 says, "Heaven and earth will disappear, but my words remain forever." Let's believe that even if we sometimes feel discouraged, God will never fail to do exactly what He's promised.

Dear Lord, thank You for promising to always do what You say You will do, no matter what. In Jesus' name, amen.

HIS PROMISE TO ADVOCATE

Because You stand up for the poor and weak, You comfort and empower them in their distress, giving them safe harbor and cool shade when it's hot; You shelter them from their oppressors' blows as a strong wall holds back the driving rain. You shelter from the relentless heat of the desert. You quiet the clamor of outsiders, ease them to stillness.

Isaiah 25:4–5 VOICE

We can all remember times when our earthly battles have left us feeling poor in spirit and weak at heart. We've all found ourselves sinking into deep distress and needing a Savior to rescue us from the pit. Being faced with oppression is just part of the human condition, and needing shelter from the heat of tough circumstances is nothing new. Each of us needs loud voices around us to be silenced from time to time. Yes, we can understand today's verses on a cellular level.

God will do this for us. He promises to be our advocate and bring much-needed relief when needed. As believers, we can count on His help when we ask for it. You are worthy of His time, energy, and love. There's no doubt about it.

Dear Lord, thank You for seeing me in the bad times and promising to meet me there. In Jesus' name, amen.

THE PROMISE TO REMOVE

At that time he will remove the cloud of gloom, the pall of death that hangs over the earth; he will swallow up death forever. The Lord God will wipe away all tears and take away forever all insults and mockery against his land and people. The Lord has spoken—he will surely do it!

Isaiah 25:7–8 TLB

This world is a tough place to live. There are so many issues coming at us daily that we can sometimes feel overwhelmed by our responsibilities and underwater in our relationships. There is grief to navigate and anxiety to work through. We worry about what the future holds while we process trauma from our past. Our insecurities often get the best of us, leaving us feeling worthless and unlovable. We have to figure out finances, meet countless deadlines, and find ways to maintain or improve our health. All this while feeling exhausted! Sometimes our emotions take control, and we get lost in them.

God promises there will come a time when He will remove the cloud of gloom and swallow up death forever. He will wipe away every tear and the pain of insults. Until then, lean into the Lord for hope, knowing that day is coming.

Dear Lord, I'm waiting with expectation.
In Jesus' name, amen.

GOD'S WORDS ARE RIGHT

For all God's words are right, and everything he does is worthy of our trust. He loves whatever is just and good; the earth is filled with his tender love.

PSALM 33:4–5 TLB

We can confidently believe the Bible to be pure and true. The words may have been penned by humans, but they were God-breathed. He inspired every word from Genesis to Revelation. In its pages, we will find what we need to live holy lives that are pleasing to the Lord. His Word is filled with promises we can anchor our hope to. He will reveal Himself through scripture so we can better understand the awe-inspiring God we serve. We can trust that all His words are right and trustworthy.

Knowing that, let's commit to time in the Word every day. Studying scripture helps believers recognize what is just and good according to the Lord. We will supernaturally experience His love as we read scripture. As we work our way through the Bible from beginning to end, our faith will grow, our hearts will be blessed, and we'll trust God as our source for all things.

Dear Lord, thank You for the promise that all Your words are right and trustworthy. Encourage me to open the Bible daily. In Jesus' name, amen.

HOPE WHILE WE WAIT

We live with hope in the Eternal. We wait for Him, for He is our Divine Help and Impenetrable Shield. Our hearts erupt with joy in Him because we trust His holy name. O Eternal, drench us with Your endless love, even now as we wait for You.

PSALM 33:20–22 VOICE

Today's verse tells us that God is our help in times of trouble, our shield when we need shelter from life's storms, is trustworthy in all things, and will love us without end every day. These are promised blessings for every believer. We can expect God's goodness in our lives, giving us hope as we wait and watch for His hand to move.

Where do you need the Lord's help to navigate your day? In what challenging circumstances do you need Him to be a shield of protection for your heart and mind? Where are you trusting Him to show up in meaningful ways? Are you desperate to know you are fully and completely loved? Talk to God and thank Him for keeping His divine promises. Tell Him what you need right now. He is listening.

Dear Lord, You are a good Father and I'm thankful for all the ways You show goodness in my life. I will wait for You with expectation. In Jesus' name, amen.

DOING GOOD

So even if you should suffer now for doing God's will, continue doing good and trust your futures to the judgment and mercy of a faithful Creator.

1 PETER 4:19 VOICE

We will suffer in the world for doing good and godly things. The Lord's will and ways are often counterintuitive to earthly expectations, so they are misunderstood by unbelievers (and even some who do believe). While we may feel like giving up and quitting when the opposition comes, we shouldn't. Today's scripture says we should continue doing good.

If the Lord asks you to further His kingdom through volunteering your time in ministry, standing up for the underdog, financially supporting underfunded programs, speaking out on behalf of the misunderstood or underserved, going against the grain, or drawing a firm line in the sand, be bold and courageous. Be His hands and feet in a broken world. Show compassion and care even when it's unpopular by worldly standards. Be an advocate where God is asking you to stand up. He promises we can confidently trust Him.

Dear Lord, embolden me to do good and godly things according to Your plan, even if it leads to my suffering. You made me and love me, and therefore I can trust my future to You. In Jesus' name, amen.

FROM EARTHLY TO ETERNAL

Dear ones, don't be surprised when you experience your trial by fire. It is not something strange and unusual, but it is something you should rejoice in. In it you share the Anointed's sufferings, and you will be that much more joyful when His glory is revealed.

1 PETER 4:12–13 VOICE

Peter is extending an invitation of sorts. He's inviting believers to shift their perspective about current trials, the ones they've already faced and the unseen ones right around the corner. Instead of feeling attacked and sorry for ourselves, we are encouraged to see these fiery trials as our participation in Jesus' sufferings.

We get to choose how we respond to life's hardships. In our lives, we'll experience everything from disease and betrayal to job loss, financial issues, and relationship trouble. If we let them, these painful trials will strengthen us until we see Him face-to-face. Having an eternal focus helps us stay resilient and endure the hardships that come our way. It's a spiritual refining process we all need to grow our faith.

If we embrace the challenge of our trials now, these verses promise that we will be happy and full of overwhelming joy when Jesus' glory is revealed.

Dear Lord, shift my perspective from earthly to eternal. In Jesus' name, amen.

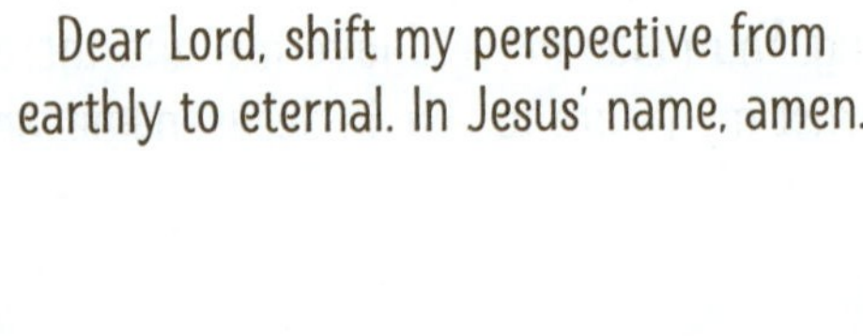

ENCASED IN HIS NAME

Then the Lord descended in the form of a pillar of cloud and stood there with him, and passed in front of him and announced the meaning of his name. "I am Jehovah, the merciful and gracious God," he said, "slow to anger and rich in steadfast love and truth."

EXODUS 34:5–6 TLB

After the first set broke, Moses prepared two more stone tablets on which God would write the Ten Commandments. He told Moses to be ready in the morning, climb to the top of Mount Sanai alone, and present himself to God. Once there, the Lord came down from the heavens in a pillar of clouds and shared powerful promises encased in His name.

Moses watched and listened as God revealed Himself, saying He is full of mercy and gracious to those who love Him. He doesn't anger easily, is patient, and is compassionate in His understanding. The Lord's love is robust and without end. It's dependable, loyal, and reliable. God is truth in every way. We can find comfort in knowing He is consistent and unchanging.

God today is the same God who appeared on the mountaintop with Moses. His promises still hold true, and they always will.

Dear Lord, I'm blessed by Your promises that hold firm and true throughout time. In Jesus' name, amen.

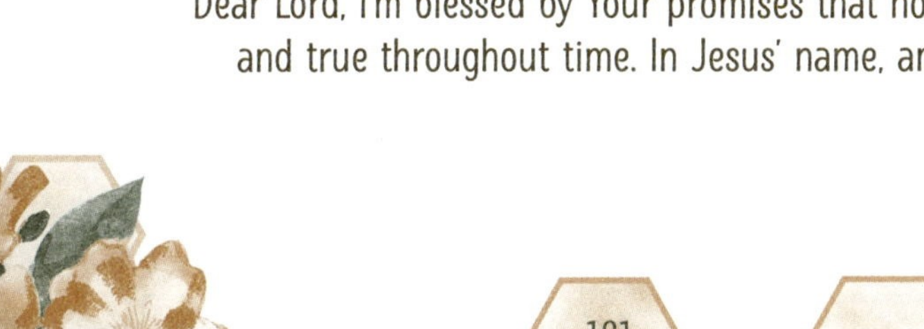

OUR UNCHANGING GOD

Jesus the Anointed One is always the same:
yesterday, today, and forever.
HEBREWS 13:8 VOICE

The only thing that will never change is the Lord, and that's a promise we can always count on. Our bank account will fluctuate, as will our job titles and salary. Relationships, family dynamics, and friendships will ebb and flow throughout our lifetime. We may feel good one day, and then our health may take a downturn the next. Seasons of life will change whether we want them to or not. We'll be forced to go with the ever-changing flow of our local, national, and world geopolitical landscape. Even our faith will change as we grow and mature. Knowing our God is the same regardless of what happens in the world should bring us comfort and peace. We can find security in His consistency. We can find hope in His dependability. We can find comfort in His reliability.

How does this knowledge affect your heart? How can His promise of steadiness bless you today? When the ever-changing things of this world stir you up, let God's promise of stability settle your anxious heart.

Dear Lord, I appreciate that You are always the same because it helps me feel secure when life continually alters and adjusts. In Jesus' name, amen.

MAGNIFICENT PROMISES

By faith Abraham's wife Sarah became fertile long after menopause because she believed God would be faithful to His promise. So from this man, who was almost at death's door, God brought forth descendants, as many as the stars in the sky and as impossible to count as the sands of the shore.

HEBREWS 11:11–12 VOICE

Sarah believed that God would fulfill His promise to make her a mother. Even at her age and stage of life, with child-bearing days long gone, this woman chose to take God at His word. She believed the impossible simply because He said it would happen. That is some kind of faith. We also have the ability to respond like Sarah and believe that God's magnificent promises will materialize in our lives.

What are you asking for that feels hopeless? What goal feels unachievable? What career path looks unworkable? What desired change appears impractical? What dream feels unfeasible? What problem seems irresolvable? What move looks ridiculous? What new medical treatment feels unviable? What opportunity looks to be unmanageable? What feels too big to walk out in faith? If God says it will happen, then it will. You can wait with confidence for the doors to open.

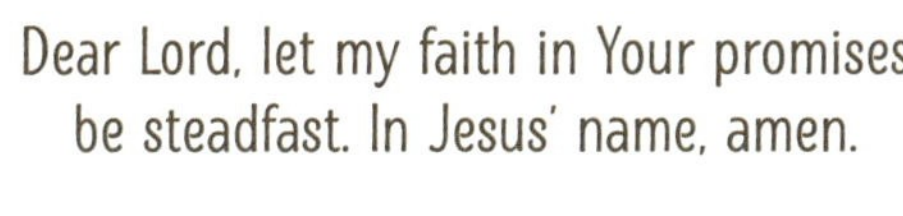

Dear Lord, let my faith in Your promises be steadfast. In Jesus' name, amen.

HALL OF FAITH

And these men of faith, though they trusted God and won his approval, none of them received all that God had promised them; for God wanted them to wait and share the even better rewards that were prepared for us.

HEBREWS 11:39–40 TLB

Often referred to as the Hall of Faith, chapter eleven in the book of Hebrews mentions several Old Testament men and women who should be commended for their faith. They weren't perfect; many failed spectacularly and had deep character flaws. When faced with the choice to trust God or themselves, however, they all chose Him. Their testimonies should encourage us as we live the life of a believer.

Interestingly, these faith-filled people who trusted God and won His approval didn't receive all that was promised. Why? Not all His plans have been completed yet. But according to today's verses, the time of fulfillment will come to pass.

If we trust like they did, we can also be included in this Hall of Faith. If we wholeheartedly place our faith in God and His promises, we will encourage those who come after us.

Dear Lord, it helps to read the stories of the faithful men and women in the Bible. They stood strong and trusted You. Let my faith in Your promises encourage others. In Jesus' name, amen.

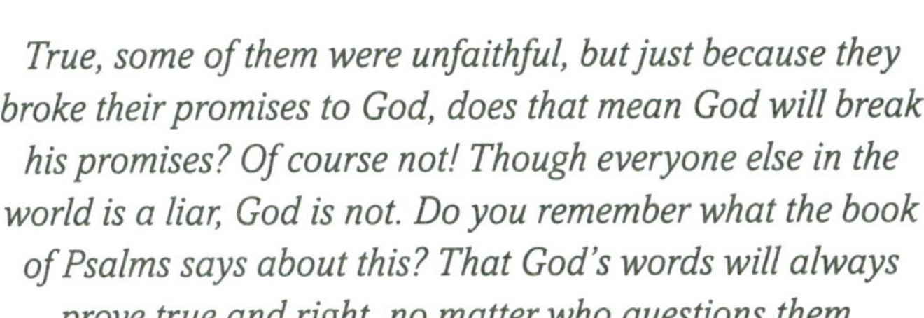

PROMISES ALWAYS KEPT

True, some of them were unfaithful, but just because they broke their promises to God, does that mean God will break his promises? Of course not! Though everyone else in the world is a liar, God is not. Do you remember what the book of Psalms says about this? That God's words will always prove true and right, no matter who questions them.

ROMANS 3:3–4 TLB

These verses remind us of God's formidable promises that we can never match or keep in return. He always follows through on His word and loves us, even when we fall short of ours. The Lord keeps His promises, and this isn't dependent on anything on our end. We can't coax it or ruin it. That is a blessing!

The good news for believers is that God won't break His vows. He simply cannot do it. They are shatterproof. We can rest assured that when the Bible mentions a divine pledge to us, it will be kept. We can anchor our hope to them. No matter how many times we fail or stumble, those promises will stand strong and be indestructible. He will bring them to fruition even when we feel unworthy.

Dear Lord, thank You for being a God of Your word! In Jesus' name, amen.

CONFIDENT ASSURANCE?

What is faith? It is the confident assurance that something we want is going to happen. It is the certainty that what we hope for is waiting for us, even though we cannot see it up ahead. Men of God in days of old were famous for their faith.

HEBREWS 11:1–2 TLB

We can have confident assurance that God hears our prayers and will provide for our needs because He says He will. Philippians 4:19 confirms this, saying "It is he who will supply all your needs from his riches in glory because of what Christ Jesus has done for us." Even though we can't see into the future, we can believe His promise to care for us. Matthew 6:31 reminds us that we don't need to worry about what we will eat, drink, or wear. God knows our needs. When we have bold faith, He will show up.

We can live with confident assurance that God will do what He says He'll do. Let's believe He knows what's best for us, even if it's different than we hoped. We can trust God without any hesitation, knowing He will grow our faith stronger through it all.

Dear Lord, I fully trust You because You're always true to Your promises. In Jesus' name, amen.

PROMISE OF A NEW BODY

Now we look forward with confidence to our heavenly bodies, realizing that every moment we spend in these earthly bodies is time spent away from our eternal home in heaven with Jesus. We know these things are true by believing, not by seeing.

2 CORINTHIANS 5:6–7 TLB

We've been promised new bodies that will be sturdy and stable for heaven. The ones we have now are weak and feeble. While we don't like to think about it, they are breaking down every day as we grow older. They will serve us here but can't go the distance. They're not meant to last forever. Chances are, you're experiencing this truth even now.

Take heart! You will have a new body in heaven, one that will be indestructible and unaffected by disease and death. Live and love well while you're here, walking out your divine calling. Don't waste time and money searching for the fountain of youth or be overly concerned with preserving yourself. Instead, be a woman of God who puts her efforts into caring for her earthly body so she can serve until Jesus calls her home.

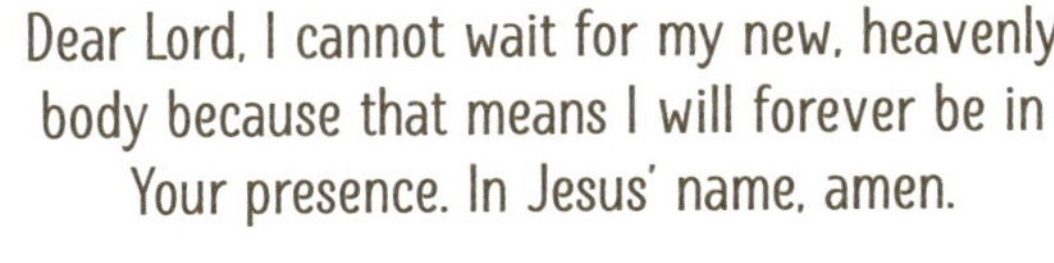

Dear Lord, I cannot wait for my new, heavenly body because that means I will forever be in Your presence. In Jesus' name, amen.

SHARING ABOUT JESUS

I have not kept Your righteousness to myself, sealed up in the secret places of my heart; instead, I boldly tell others how You save and how loyal You are. I haven't been shy to talk about Your love, nor have I been afraid to tell Your truth before the great assembly of Your people.

PSALM 40:10 VOICE

The psalmist sets an excellent example that believers should follow today. Instead of keeping God's goodness concealed and to himself, he proclaimed it to those around him. He shared the good news with others, talking about how the Lord is a promise keeper. Why is this important? Because word of mouth is a powerful endorsement.

Be bold when you tell people about what God has done. Let them know how He's been good to you. Talk about the ways He has blessed you at the right time and in the right ways. Share what you're learning about the Lord through time in the Word. Unpack your testimony and how you've seen God's promises play out in your life. Don't be shy or intimidated. Instead, ask for open doors of opportunity and the courage to walk through them.

Dear Lord, embolden me to be Your spokesperson in this dark world. In Jesus' name, amen.

GOD THINKS OF YOU

But may all who look for You discover true joy and happiness in You; may those who cherish how You save them always say, "O Eternal One, You are great and are first in our hearts." Meanwhile, I am empty and need so much, but I know the Lord is thinking of me. You are my help; only You can save me, my True God. Please hurry.

PSALM 40:16–17 VOICE

Have you ever considered that the God who created the heavens and the earth and everything in between thinks of you? With everything going on in the world, with millions simultaneously praying different prayers, with wars and disasters and sicknesses abounding, God is still thinking of you. You're always on His mind.

Let that sink in and bring you joy. Let it encourage you to know you're deeply loved and cherished. Be blessed knowing God sees you and saves you. When He makes promises to believers, they always come to pass.

Take time today to thank the Lord for His faithfulness. Thank Him for never letting you out of His focus. Let Him know how much you love Him in return.

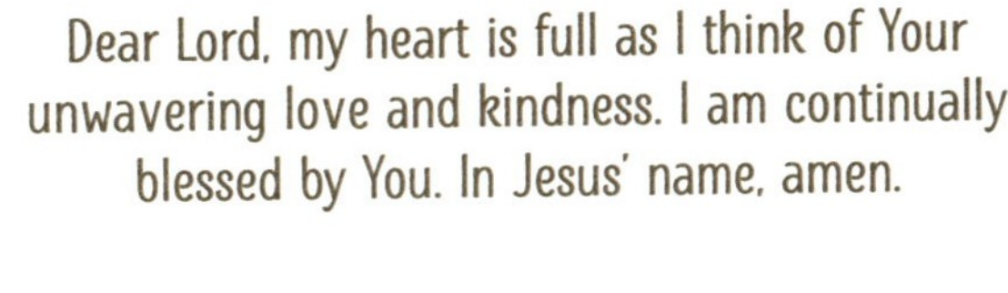

Dear Lord, my heart is full as I think of Your unwavering love and kindness. I am continually blessed by You. In Jesus' name, amen.

PROMISED TO BELIEVERS

Your steadfast love, O Lord, is as great as all the heavens. Your faithfulness reaches beyond the clouds. Your justice is as solid as God's mountains. Your decisions are as full of wisdom as the oceans are with water. You are concerned for men and animals alike.

PSALM 36:5–6 TLB

God promises to provide these to every believer: steadfast love, faithfulness, justice, wisdom, and care. We can trust them to be part of our Christian life, never based on what we do but on who He is. Without a doubt, God is a generous Father.

Consider how these promises have played out in your life. Remembering how and where the Lord has revealed Himself can help grow your trust and confidence that He'll do it again.

Think about it. When was the last time you were fully aware of God's steadfast love? In what circumstances has He been undeniably faithful? Have you seen the Lord's justice prevail in significant and timely ways? When has much-needed wisdom rushed into your thoughts and you knew it was divine? In what challenging situations did you feel His care and concern?

Dear Lord, as I think about the times You have shown up, I'm humbled. You always prove Yourself trustworthy and faithful. Thank You. In Jesus' name, amen.

UNFAILING LOVE AND BLESSINGS

For you are the Fountain of life; our light is from your light. Pour out your unfailing love on those who know you! Never stop giving your blessings to those who long to do your will.

PSALM 36:9–10 TLB

God promises His children unfailing love. He promises blessings will be poured out on those who pursue and follow His will. The Lord promises to shine through us into a dark world that needs to know Jesus. It's through Him that we are given eternal life in heaven.

If we really embraced this truth, we would be on fire for the Lord every day. It would fuel and embolden us to share our testimony with others. Our words and actions would reveal faith that His promises will never fail. We'd walk with a spring in our step and genuine confidence in knowing we're fully and completely loved. We'd want to tell others about God's promises that are available to them. Does this describe you?

It can be challenging to live in such freedom, even for the most seasoned believer. Just believing we're loved so deeply can be hard at times! Ask God to make His promises come alive in your heart.

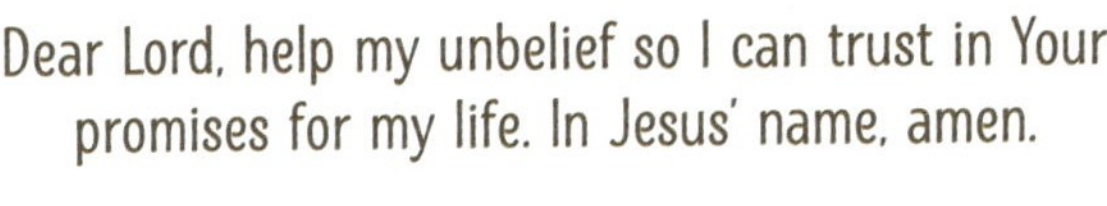

Dear Lord, help my unbelief so I can trust in Your promises for my life. In Jesus' name, amen.

GOD'S WORD SPEAKS

Forever, O Lord, your Word stands firm in heaven. Your faithfulness extends to every generation, like the earth you created; it endures by your decree, for everything serves your plans.

PSALM 119:89–91 TLB

The psalmist is stressing here that God's Word always speaks to His faithfulness. It stands strongly against every argument meant to disqualify because scripture is permanent and unchanging. We can trust it to be a firm foundation in our lives. Each verse we read is God-breathed and will continue to stand the test of time. Every promise revealed has or will come to pass. As believers, we will always be able to find wisdom, encouragement, direction, and comfort in its pages. But for that to happen, we must pull our Bible off the shelf, dust it off, and open it daily. That's how we will reap the benefits it offers.

What keeps you from reading the Bible every day? Knowing it's a living document of God's goodness, why is it difficult to commit to digging in? Can you remember a time when you felt the Lord speak to you through its pages? We need constant reminders of His faithfulness. They give us hope for today.

Dear Lord, there's nothing else that will bring blessings like time in Your Word. In Jesus' name, amen.

INVEST IN THE WORD

Nothing is perfect except your words. Oh, how I love them.
I think about them all day long. They make me wiser
than my enemies because they are my constant guide.
Yes, wiser than my teachers, for I am ever thinking of
your rules. They make me even wiser than the aged.

PSALM 119:96–100 TLB

Today's verses promise that the more we invest in reading the Bible, the wiser we become. The psalmist knows the awesome power that's buried in God's Word and how it is supernaturally released into our lives when we read it. He knows there's guidance in the Word, so he will be smarter than any enemy he encounters. As he digs through scripture, it will make him more knowledgeable than his teachers or even those older than him.

Did you know that promise is also for us today? The Bible teaches us to live better—this is why we should read it daily. We learn ways to live in victory. It helps us make good and godly choices. The Word's transformative power changes us from the inside out.

Dear Lord, thank You for Your Word and the power it has to make me more like Jesus. I'm committed to being in it every day. In Jesus' name, amen.

GOD WILL GUIDE YOU

We do not doubt the Lord's intentions for you; we are confident that you are carrying out, and will continue to carry out, the commands we are sending your way. May the Lord guide your hearts into God's pure love and keep you headed straight into the strong and sure grip of the Anointed One.

2 THESSALONIANS 3:4–5 VOICE

When we seek God's help to pursue a righteous life, the Holy Spirit will direct our steps and bring us comfort. We can believe that with confidence. The more we press into our relationship with Him, the more we will connect to His restorative love. We can run to Him when our hearts are heavy with grief, and He will embrace us. He will meet us in our brokenness and bring hope in our weariness. In God's love, we will find the wisdom to navigate both the mountaintops and valleys of life with integrity and grace. We will be strengthened to stand tall when persecution comes our way. We will be quick to cling to the Lord when confusion keeps us from seeing clearly.

His promise to keep us close and meet our needs will be our guiding light in the darkness.

Dear Lord, I need Your love today more than ever. In Jesus' name, amen.

HIS WORDS ARE EVERGREEN

My words are always true and always here with you. Heaven and earth will pass away, but My words will never pass away.
MATTHEW 24:35 VOICE

Today's scripture boldly promises that God's Word will stand the test of time. We may say something one minute and then forget it the next. We may vow to do something with every good intention, and then let it keep sliding down our to-do list. We might try to bring a pledge to fruition but find ourselves unable to follow through. Our words carry little weight next to the Lord's, and that is important to keep in mind.

When Jesus said that His words are *always true and always here*, it was a blessing few, if any, recognized at the time. The encouragement they brought to the disciples, and then to the Gentiles, and then passed down through countless generations to you, is still true. God's promises made then are still here today, alive and active in believers' lives. They will be fulfilled in those who come next. His words are evergreen, more than we can imagine.

Dear Lord, what a blessing to spend time with Your precious Word. I am grateful that it's just as true today as it was back then. In Jesus' name, amen.

HELP IN FOLLOWING

Loving God means doing what he tells us to do, and really, that isn't hard at all; for every child of God can obey him, defeating sin and evil pleasure by trusting Christ to help him.

1 JOHN 5:3–4 TLB

We can trust the Lord to help us love Him better. He will empower us through the Holy Spirit to do what He tells us to do and live how He wants us to live. There is nothing He may ask that we cannot do with His help and guidance. Even in our flawed state and our imperfect condition, we're able to please the Lord by living with a holy purpose. He promises to help us follow His commands.

As we read through the Word, God speaks to believers, bringing encouragement and wisdom. We will find comfort through its pages and practical ways we can show our love in action. We'll find the strength to forgive as commanded, especially when it feels impossible. Our faith will grow each time we choose to obey God's leading. We will be blessed by it supernaturally.

Dear Lord, when I ask for help, I know You will always give me the strength, wisdom, and guidance to do what You've commanded. In Jesus' name, amen.

THE PROTECTION OF GOD

We all know that everyone fathered by God will not make sin a way of life because God protects His children from the evil one, and the evil one can't touch them. Have confidence in the fact that we belong to God, but also know that the world around us is in the grips of the evil one.

1 JOHN 5:18–19 VOICE

God promises to watch over His children. When Jesus becomes our Savior, we will find ourselves fully loved and surrounded by God's protection. James 1:17 tells us we will receive good and perfect gifts from God. Matthew 11:29–30 says Jesus will carry our burdens so we can find rest. And according to John 16:13–15, the Holy Spirit will guide us according to the Father's truth and His will for our lives. As believers, we are encased in God's goodness in every way from the moment we secure our saving faith through eternity.

This beautiful truth is why we won't make sin a way of life. The enemy will come at us through the ways of the world, but we're secure in Jesus. We won't be perfect in our pursuit of righteous living, but we're surrounded by God's promises that won't ever fail or falter.

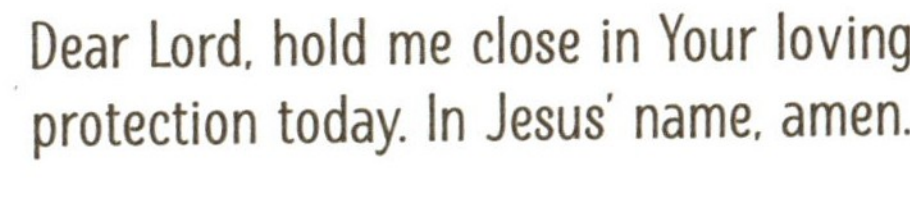

Dear Lord, hold me close in Your loving protection today. In Jesus' name, amen.

NO MATTER HOW DEEP

Come, let's talk this over, says the Lord; no matter how deep the stain of your sins, I can take it out and make you as clean as freshly fallen snow. Even if you are stained as red as crimson, I can make you white as wool! If you will only let me help you, if you will only obey, then I will make you rich!

ISAIAH 1:18–19 TLB

There is no sin that Jesus' blood can't wash away. There's nothing you've done that can't be made clean. Many think they've sinned too much or have done something too egregious to receive forgiveness. This kind of thinking is what keeps some people from accepting Jesus as their personal Savior. They think they've got to clean themselves up first before surrendering to the Lord and receiving eternal forgiveness. When they can't, they live in defeat and never experience the promises of God.

Scripture is clear that no matter how deep the stains of your sins, He can—and He will—remove them. You are redeemable by the one who holds the whole world in His hands.

Dear Lord, I feel so unworthy of Your love. I've made so many mistakes. Thank You for the gift of forgiveness, even forgiveness for the deepest stains of my sins. In Jesus' name, amen.

THE PROMISE OF BLESSED

While he was saying these things, some woman lifted her voice above the murmur of the crowd: "Blessed the womb that carried you, and the breasts at which you nursed!" Jesus commented, "Even more blessed are those who hear God's Word and guard it with their lives!"

LUKE 11:27–28 MSG

Being blessed is the kind of happiness that comes from receiving God's favor. It's experiencing the fullness of His presence in our lives every day of the week. It's a fully satisfied soul rather than a wealth of material items. It's our inner state of well-being because of our relationship with the Lord. It comes from being in a deep fellowship with Him. We're blessed by surrendering our will to His.

How do we walk this out? When we make spending time in the Word a daily priority, it blesses us. As we let scripture ruminate in our hearts as we go about our day, we are blessed. As we put into action what we've read in the Bible, we receive the promise of God's blessings.

The life of a believer should be marked by the promise of blessing. How do you see it coming to fruition in yours?

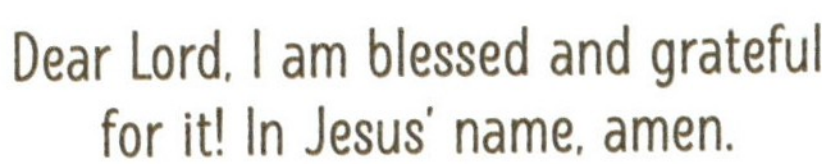

Dear Lord, I am blessed and grateful
for it! In Jesus' name, amen.

GOD EQUIPS THE CALLED

Look! I am going to send a heavenly messenger before you to protect you during your journey and lead you safely to the place I have prepared for you. . . . If you are obedient to his voice and follow all of My instructions, then I will be an enemy to all of those who are against you, and I will oppose all those who oppose you.

Exodus 23:20, 22 voice

God pledged to provide a heavenly messenger to protect the Israelites' entry into Canaan, the Promised Land. Their clear instructions were to drive the current inhabitants out, destroy their places of worship, and serve only God. This may have felt like a big request, but it was doable. Why? Because He also promised that their obedience would be rewarded with His steadfast protection against everyone who opposed them.

Believers today can be certain that when God asks us to follow His lead, there will be a blessing for doing so. What He promises will happen without fail. While there may be times when what He asks feels too big, He will equip us to accomplish His requests.

Dear Lord, I appreciate the reminder that You don't call the equipped. Instead, You equip the called. There's help in the moment and a promise on the other side. In Jesus' name, amen.

GOD DRAWS CLOSE

Anyone who loves Me will listen to My voice and obey. The Father will love him, and We will draw close to him and make a dwelling place within him.

John 14:23 VOICE

When we decide to follow the Lord and accept Jesus as our Savior, He promises that He will draw close to us. In that moment, God's Holy Spirit will take up residency in us as a constant companion. The Spirit will enable us to hear and obey what's asked of us for righteous living.

There is no greater gift on earth than to have God's presence as we navigate the difficulties of this world. We may try to find help and hope here, but every earthly option will leave us wanting. There's no substitute that even comes close to what God offers.

He brings comfort in the face of life's storms, wisdom and discernment amid confusion, and peace instead of chaos. The Lord draws close to those who love Him and are purposeful in pursuing a right relationship. His presence is a promise.

Dear Lord, draw close and enable me to hear Your voice and obey. I value Your presence in my life! In Jesus' name, amen.

PUTTING THE WORD INTO ACTION

For if a person just listens and doesn't obey, he is like a man looking at his face in a mirror; as soon as he walks away, he can't see himself anymore or remember what he looks like. But if anyone keeps looking steadily into God's law for free men, he will not only remember it but he will do what it says, and God will greatly bless him in everything he does.

JAMES 1:23–25 TLB

We grow in our faith and closer to the Lord by reading the Bible. The more we dig into scripture, meditating on its wisdom, the more equipped we are to live a righteous life. We read about how we can delight God with our words and actions. We understand how He empowers us to live and love others well. We learn about forgiveness and why it's imperative for believers. The Word reveals the goodness of God and what makes Him a faithful Father. It instructs us on how to be women with steadfast faith.

If we choose to ignore this insight, we'll remain bound by our sinful nature. But if we read and remember, putting what we've learned into action, He promises to bless us in meaningful and significant ways.

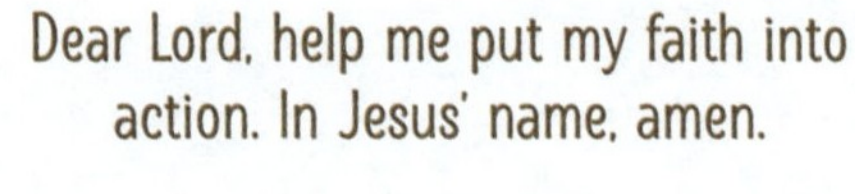

RIGHT AND RECONCILED LIFE

Doesn't it make sense that if you sign yourself over as a slave, you will have to obey your master? The question before you is, What will be your master? Will it be sin—which will lead to certain death—or obedience—which will lead to a right and reconciled life?

Romans 6:16 voice

Paul challenges us to choose between sin and obedience, understanding that they both lead to different outcomes. We are faced daily with decisions that will clearly reveal what rules us. If we become slaves to our fleshly desires, which lead us into sinful behavior, we'll face the destruction of ourselves and what we hold dear. But if we choose to obey God, the promise is a right and reconciled life.

On paper, the choice is obvious. Why would anyone want to act in ways that might destroy their life? But the reality is that the heart wants what the heart wants, making it a grueling decision to obey God instead. That's why we need the Lord to strengthen us to follow Him as an act of surrender.

Dear Lord, help me want You more than my own fleshly desires. Remind me that obedience leads to a right and reconciled life in You. That is what I want. In Jesus' name, amen.

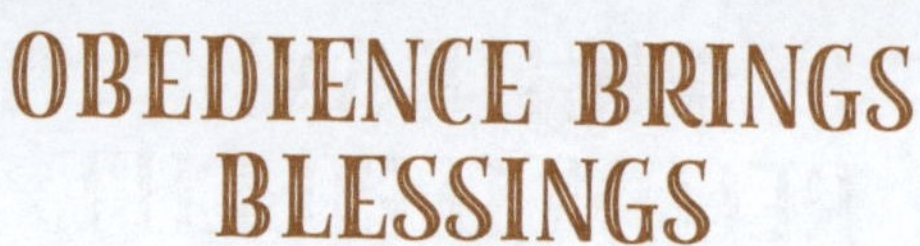

OBEDIENCE BRINGS BLESSINGS

I wanted them to trust Me and obey My voice. In those early days, I told them, "I will be your God, and you will be My people. Follow Me every step of the way into a life that is good." But they didn't trust Me. They didn't obey My voice. They refused to listen to Me. Instead they followed the plans of their own stubborn hearts. Each step was a step backward, not forward.

JEREMIAH 7:23–24 VOICE

Obedience is a big deal to God. It's not because He's an egomaniac who needs to be worshipped to feel better about Himself. He isn't a micromanager wanting to boss us around. Instead, God desires obedience from believers because it keeps us out of trouble. When we follow His guidance, it keeps our feet on the path of righteousness, which leads to blessings. It steers us into a good life. This is a promise.

When we don't obey and choose to follow our own plan, we'll find ourselves tangled in all sorts of knots. It's like we've taken steps away from God, going backward instead of forward in faith.

Dear Lord, help me be a woman of faith who delights in obeying Your will and ways, reaping with gratitude the blessings that come from it. In Jesus' name, amen.

AN ETERNITY IN HEAVEN

Not everyone who says to Me, "Lord, Lord," will enter the kingdom of heaven. Simply calling Me "Lord" will not be enough. Only those who do the will of My Father who is in heaven will join Me in heaven.

MATTHEW 7:21 VOICE

If we love the Lord and have a saving faith, our desire will be to follow God's commands. We won't do so perfectly by any means, nor are we expected to. But if we try to walk righteously with purpose and passion, it will please Him. Our intentionality to live good and godly lives will be noticed. When our priority is to obey as an expression of our genuine faith, we're promised an eternity in heaven—not because of our works, but because of a saving faith that prompts our pursuit of righteous living.

How does this challenge you today? Is your eternity secured in heaven? If you're not sure, pray this prayer right now:

Dear Lord, I repent of my sins and surrender my life into Your hands. Jesus is God's one and only Son who died on the cross for my sins and rose again three days later. I believe in my heart and confess with my mouth that Jesus is my Savior. In His name I pray, amen.

THE PROMISE OF BLESSING

Praise the Lord! For all who fear God and trust in him are blessed beyond expression. Yes, happy is the man who delights in doing his commands.

PSALM 112:1 TLB

If we fear God, respect Him in reverent awe, and trust in Him for help and hope, we will be blessed in abundance. When we spend time in the Word, learning His commands for righteous living and then putting them into action, we will be deeply delighted.

Trusting God is challenging for many, especially when life feels out of control. We've trusted people in the past and seen it end badly. Rather than recognize His awesomeness and wait with expectation for His goodness to show itself, we try to fix things ourselves. We turn to the world instead of calling out to God. We follow our own path rather than God's plan. As a result, we end up stressed more than blessed.

There is hope! Open your heart and let the Lord's promises inform and direct your relationship with Him. Learn to surrender your will to His. When you do, peace and joy will overflow.

Dear Lord, I confess my personal struggle to trust others. Help me rely on You, for You're a good and faithful Father! In Jesus' name, amen.

THE PROMISE OF CONSTANT CARE

Such a man will not be overthrown by evil circumstances. God's constant care of him will make a deep impression on all who see it. He does not fear bad news, nor live in dread of what may happen. For he is settled in his mind that Jehovah will take care of him. That is why he is not afraid but can calmly face his foes.

PSALM 112:6–8 TLB

Talk about holy confidence! The writer is assured that God is in control and will provide constant care for him. Even more, the psalmist is excited to think of how that will encourage those who see God's hand of protection. He's not worried about an unknown future. He doesn't fear a dreaded phone call with sad news. He isn't concerned that calamity may come his way. His faith is anchored by God's promise to take care of him no matter what.

What about you? Maybe you're a notorious worrier who stresses over things that will probably never happen. But living a life of faith means trusting God in every circumstance, allowing us to stay calm in the chaos.

Dear Lord, what a relief that You provide me with constant care so I can experience peace. In Jesus' name, amen.

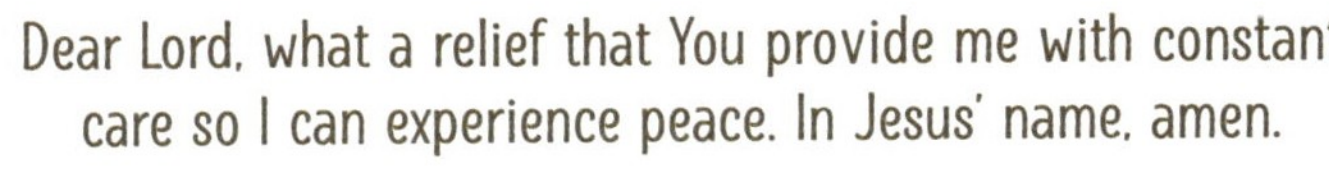

HE LOVED US FIRST

My commandment to you is this: love others as I have loved you. There is no greater way to love than to give your life for your friends. You celebrate our friendship if you obey this command.

JOHN 15:12–14 VOICE

God's greatest command is for us to love Him with all our heart, soul, mind, and strength. Secondly, we're to love others as ourselves. The only reason we can live these out daily is because God made good on His promise to love us first. Our ability to love comes from Him. The Lord's abundant love spills out of us and onto others.

But sometimes, we don't feel capable of loving well. We're annoyed at the behavior of others or see them as a constant source of drama. They think differently than we do about key topics like faith and politics. They're reckless in how they treat others, or they insert themselves into our business. Loving them seems impossible.

Ask God to open your heart so you can see these people through His eyes. Ask for an extra measure of compassion so you can release offenses and forgive them. Ask the Lord to remind you of His promise to love so that you can love too.

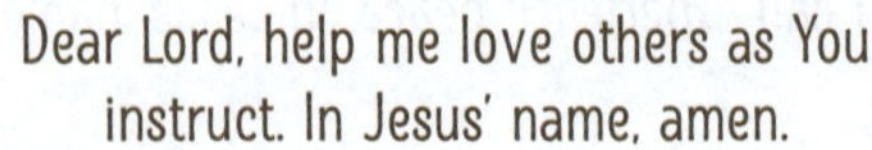

Dear Lord, help me love others as You instruct. In Jesus' name, amen.

SCRIPTURE INDEX

OLD TESTAMENT

NEW TESTAMENT

Matthew

Luke

John

Acts

Romans

1 Corinthians

2 Corinthians